AF282345

Petra Bouren
in cooperation with the
Annual group "Christian Family
Constellation"

We have a God who heals!

Concept of family constellations on a Christian basis

<u>Imprint:</u>

Bibliographic information of the German National Library:
The Deutsche Nationalbibliothek lists this publication in the
Deutsche Nationalbibliografie; detailed bibliographical
Data is available on the Internet at <u>http://dnb.dnb.de.</u>

© 2023 Petra Bouren
Publishing:
BoD · Books on Demand GmbH, Überseering 33,
22297 Hamburg, bod@bod.de
Printing:
Libri Plureos GmbH, Friedensallee 273, 22763 Hamburg
ISBN: 978-3-7578-0433-6

Foreword

*"A vision becomes a reality when I
have the courage,
to go beyond my limits."*

Lena Meichsner

How I came to write this book

Keep watch over your heart
with all care;
so you will have life
(Proverbs 4:23)

It was a very moving moment for me at the end of January 2016, when I said goodbye to the training group after two and a half years of training as a family constellator with Dr. Victor Chu in Neckargemünd. I was in the starting blocks to put what I had learned into practice. My trainer, Dr. Victor Chu, confirmed me in my abilities. He commissioned and blessed me for the task that now lay ahead of me. He encouraged me to implement my project, a year group "Family Constellations in the Christian realm". His saying: "I am curious to see where you will be in three years" has motivated me ever since and gives me strength for this project.

The months of March and April 2016 were "practice months" in my circle of friends. It was a time when I was confronted in many conversations with questions like these: "Is family constellation even compatible with our faith? What about constellating people who have already died?" The more I dealt with people and their thoughts as well as their questions, the more often I answered them, the more my own concept of the "Christian Family Constellations" developed. My ideas of family constellations based on Christian and biblical thinking, which I present in this book, became clearer and clearer. It became clearer and clearer to me what I would like to pass on.

On 10 May 2016 I went public with my constellation work. I invited through the church association KAB (Catholic Workers' Movement) to an open evening to "get to know Christian family constellations", which was attended by 17 people. Again I was confronted with many questions. Also from this evening many conversations developed. I encouraged the participants to take part in the "taster evenings" in the next two months in order to get to know my way of working. After another open evening in September, I offered the first block of the annual group "Christian Family Constellations" starting in October 2016.

As I continued to "move forward", a new project developed: "Family Constellations in the Forge", which I now offer together with my friend Petra on their farm. The participants come primarily from the church sector. New questions arose: "What is the difference between traditional family constellations and Christian family constellations? What is "Christian" about your constellation work? Can family constellations also be found in the Bible or what does the Bible say about it?" The new suggestions challenged me to deal with these thoughts as well.

People kept asking me, "Why don't you write a book?" The thought never left my mind. And now I'm going to do it! It is a very personal book. Mosaic pieces from conversations I've had flow into it, questions I've encountered again and again over the past year. David serves as an example from the Bible. My own experiences with family constellations, as well as experiences I have had together with the year group within the past year, serve as inspiration for the book. It is a collaborative project, as the participants from our group have agreed to let others share their experiences with "Christian Family Constellations". The participants report their own experiences on the individual topics within family constellations (for their own protection under someone else's name). Some topics also appear in my book that did not arise within our group, but which I have included from the time of my training. For reasons of readability, I generally use the masculine form; of course, this also always refers to the female participants.

Family constellation has brought a lot of healing into my life. I am a Christian and have a personal relationship with Jesus. My concept "Christian Family Constellation" is built on this foundation. It is my concern to let this possibility of healing flow into our Christian and church circles. I am convinced that God is working in our lives and wants healing for us. In the constellations I have experienced again and again that God touches the soul of the human being, gives insight and heals.

With my book I want to make my own, newly developed concept known and help Christians to get their own picture of family constellations.

Introduction:

On the road together

"All that is real in life is encounter."

Dr. Martin Buber

Annual Group "Christian Family Constellations"

I understand family constellations as a process that takes place over a longer period of time. A group that meets regularly once a month in a protected setting is suitable for this. The evening begins with an impulse, i.e. a story for reflection. In the exchange that follows, each person can share what the past constellation has done for him or her or what is currently on his or her mind. One family constellation takes place per evening. Not only my "own constellation" has an effect on my life, but from every constellation I experience I can find aspects in my life. At the end there is a "flash light": everyone shares in short words how they are feeling at the moment. What has happened is rounded off, the bag is "tied" before going home. The evening ends with a summarizing and concluding prayer.

In order to give each other a protected framework, it is important that what happens in the group stays in the group. Everyone who chooses to participate in such a group commits to the confidentiality. For a dynamic group process it is important that the participants attend the meetings in a binding manner, that means participating regularly. A binding group enables familiarity and openness. One walks a common path with each other in a protected setting, whereby everyone decides the speed of their own process.

Usually a family constellation is only the beginning of a process. As a participant I may go home with the knowledge that the constellation only shows as much as the family system and the constellating person themselves allow. However, a single constellation is usually not enough to untie the knots of a life. Further constellations are necessary. They reveal new aspects, new perspectives from a different angle.

The protected framework, the accompanied process, is important for the method of family constellations, since the process of looking at and then stepping out of the previous family structures is a profound process. I would like to take thoughts from the film "Titanic" as an example. The main character Rose, from a venerable English family but now impoverished family, is supposed to marry one of the richest men in England to save her family. However, she does not love this man. In desperation, she wants to throw herself over the railing to escape the whole situation. In the process, she is "seen" by a penniless young painter who persuades her to climb back down from the railing. She falls in love with him, as she feels perceived by him and "seen" as she really is. This gives her the strength to break away from conventional family structures and start a new life under a new identity in America, even without her "savior". With the Titanic had to sink an entire ship for Rose to break free from the rigid structures of her family of origin.

This stepping out of the old structures causes fear. We are confronted with feelings like fear, anger, powerlessness and pain. With the things from our old life, which we have, until now "covered", pushed aside and repressed. It is not an easy process. The steps on new ground are still shaky and uncertain, but there I would like to call out to the reader with the song of "Youth with a Mission": "Take in, take in the good land that God gives you". You don't have to walk the path alone, HE goes the way with you and puts people at your side (for example through a year group) who choose a similar way and therefore also understand you within your process of change.

<u>Josefa:</u>

I have very good friends who have told me again and again about the year group, and also about how important these evenings are for them, because they offer the opportunity to come to terms with one's own life story. Through this exchange, our conversations took on a new quality and depth. At some point the idea came up that I should also take part in such an evening. With the invitation, the friend gave me the feeling that he wanted to give me a gift.

In my life, until recently, no performance requirement was too much. I had the idea that I could do and manage everything. But I am a "unfree" perfectionist. At some point my heart said, "I can't go on like this". I could no longer climb a mountain, climb any stairs without getting out of breath.

A conversation with a friend made me think about what the word "breathless" means in my life and what could be the background for my heart complaints. I researched on the internet and found out that heart complaints indicate unresolved conflicts within the family, the partnership or other areas of life. The breathlessness showed that there is a need to pause, to look inward from the outside.

At this point, when I encountered the possibility of a family constellation through my friends, I knew this was my path. On the first evening I was very excited, as I always am when I meet people I don't know or find myself in situations that are new and that I can't assess. At the same time, I felt secure because my friends were also a part of the group. I found that it wasn't just my friends that made me feel safe, but that there was a respectful, trusting, and loving demeanor in the group that made my fears disappear. After that evening, I decided that the long journey (200 km) was worth it.

I feel very comfortable within the year group because I was able to get to know people in a way that is rarely possible otherwise. It's not about looking good, it's about developing. At the same time, my confidence is high that I am also carried in the group with uncomfortable feelings such as powerlessness, fear, anger, vulnerability, insecurities and so forth.

Part I:

Christian Family Constellation

"Let's start being who we want to be."

The common thread in my life

My love for you is an eternal love,
so with mercy I have made you
come with me
(Jeremiah 31:3)

I was born in 1959, at the end of the 1950s, in the post-war period, a time of reconstruction. Both my parents had lived through the war and now it was time to build something. My mother had little household money to provide for the family as it all went into our business, vines and fields. Land ownership was very important in those days. "Schaffe, schaffe Häusle baue.", work, work, work, was the motto of our family. Our everyday life was marked by work. We had a glazing shop and it was a matter of course that I was the "second man" behind the machines in the afternoons after school and that my mother helped on the building site. There was no time for dates with friends or hobbies. When I started my apprenticeship as a bank clerk in 1977, someone was hired in our glazing shop to replace me. My brothers, who were born in the 60s, experienced their childhood in a completely different way.

My apprenticeship in a bank was a very enjoyable time for me: we were like one big family. Even today, I still maintain good contacts with my former colleagues. After my apprenticeship, in the summer of 1980, I had the opportunity to take unpaid leave. I worked for three months in Zermatt (Switzerland) in a restaurant. It was a time of freedom and new experiences. I suddenly had friends and could enjoy the time with other young people. Every day in the evening a group met in the restaurant where I worked. It was not long before I was also part of this group. A young person from our group from Zermatt was sent by his hotel for some time to the

"Hörnlihütte" a hut at the foot of the Matterhorn. Nevertheless, in order to meet with us as a group, he set off late in the evening for Zermatt, despite bad weather. He "fell into the depths" on the descent into the village.

The death of this friend led me into a severe life crisis. Our group broke up. I vacillated between returning to the bank in Germany and taking a job in Zermatt. Even at home with my parents, there were conflicts. Why did God allow this? I had friends for the first time in my life and now Franky's death was taking that community away from me. When my mother asked me on the afternoon of December 24, 1980, if I didn't want to go to confession, all my rebellion against God burst out of me. I blamed Him for everything: for Franky's death and for my present situation. This invitation to confession, however, left me no peace. Just before the end of the confession time, I took my bicycle and rode to the church. There, in preparation for confession, I placed the shambles of my life into Jesus' hands. Since then, I have seen Jesus' guidance in my life like a red thread.

I went back to Zermatt were I experienced my first steps in faith during my stay there. We were a group of about 60 people between the ages of 15 and 91 who met every Monday for the "Bible and Prayer" prayer group. We young people in particular experienced a very beautiful fellowship with one another, went skiing together, we took part in various Christian meetings together. We were very happy to be able to share our prayers with others in Switzerland, and we loved singing Christian songs together. Often the worship of our prayer evening continued afterwards in one of Zermatt's inns, which did not particularly please the landlords.

In 1983, five participants in our prayer group, including myself, attended a "Discipleship Training School" (short Bible school with an emphasis on evangelism) together from "Youth with a Mission" in Biel. A time followed in which I was able to experience God's blessing in my life. A time in which many gifts and abilities could show themselves and develop in my life. I discovered my heart for children, began training as a catechist, worked and lived within a parish community in Valais and helped to build up a prayer group within the parish. I loved the mountains and Switzerland; however, the Swiss authorities threw a wrench in my life plans. My work permit was not renewed. I could not continue and finish my training as a catechist, and I had to leave Switzerland.

This was followed by a one-year internship in a religious hospital. I was confronted with illness and death, attended a seminar on dying and had conversations with many dying people in their last days in relation to faith. With one of the nuns I could always talk about individual patients and their process.

My path led me back to my former working-place in the bank. In my free time I built up a prayer group with a vicar. Together we conducted various faith seminars in our area.

During this time I participated in a ski camp of "Youth with a Mission" in Adelboden (Switzerland). At our prayer evening during the ski camp I received the following impulse, for me a clear promise: God has a plan for my life, he will use me in a greater measure than I can imagine myself.

These thoughts reminded me of my childhood, of my First Communion preparation, where our priest led me to Jesus. I can still remember the moment when I returned from communion to the pew and placed my life in Jesus' hands. The desire to go on mission had been growing in my heart since my Communion. This desire, after this promise, took more and more shape, that is, to live as a family in the mission, if possible within the Catholic Church.

When I got to know the ICPE (International Catholic Program for Evangelization) "Allerheiligen" in the Black Forest in the winter of 1990, I thought I had found my place. That winter I spent every weekend within the ICPE community and then decided to attend a two-year staff training course. I was in a relationship at the time, which I dissolved because my boyfriend at the time couldn't imagine going down such a path with me. My supervisor at the bank was not pleased when I resigned, as three women were pregnant at the time and he desperately needed me. He made it clear to me that if I left now, I could not come back easily. I gave up my apartment and pulled up stakes behind me. At the end of February 1991 I took my mother with me to "Allerheiligen" in order to gently teach her that I would be going there from April 1991. She could not and would not accept this. In addition, during this time, in one and the same night, my uncle was killed in a traffic accident and my paternal grandmother died. For a month, until I moved to Allerheiligen, my mother woke me up every night to complain to me that she couldn't handle all of this. The telephone conversation always ended with her prophesying that I would come back from Allerheilligen after all.

After two years, to my mother's delight, I actually returned to "normal life" while my father felt the pain of it in me and he met me in it.

I buried my dream for missions and also the thought that God wanted to use me. I found a job in public service, where I still work today (till my pension 2023).

At the age of 40 I got married. My desire was to have a family and children, with a partner at my side with whom I could also live my faith. Two years later my daughter was born, who gives me a lot of joy.

Unfortunately, I couldn't do what was important to me in my marriage. My marriage fell apart.

At 50, I grappled with the painful thought that God's promise to use me in a greater measure in my life has not become reality. By now I was probably too old for it, I thought.

So during these years I sought help in the pastoral area, but I experienced again and again that I got stuck at a certain point and did not get any further. For years I had the feeling of running into a wall again and again, despite good pastoral support. A colleague and friend showed me the way of family constellations. So my way led me to Neckargemünd to Dr. Victor Chu. Together with my counsellor I formulated my questions. The causes of my difficulties were clear, but I wanted a solution, yes, a resolution of these difficulties in my life.

The Wall

You tear down all my walls and
cause my strongholds to
crumble!
(Psalm 89:40)

The family constellation was the breakthrough in my life. The wall was torn down. I could experience:
"You Lord, you break down all my walls and cause my strongholds to crumble!" Not that everything changed from one moment to the next - not that. But the constellation gave me the tools to tackle my difficulties. My solution picture in the constellation was "detachment". Wherever I apply this solution picture to difficult situations in my life, I experience "entanglements" being released. With this picture, which I painted in 2011, I tried to express my experience with family constellation: The wall was broken through the cross and the love of God, as well as the covenant of God that accompanies me on the path of healing.

After experiencing another breakthrough and healing in another constellation three years later, I decided to train with Dr. Victor Chu. This led me into a new, very enriching phase of my life. It is not always easy, but I feel carried. The healing love of God is present for me. Family constellations opened the door to new perspectives and new ways of seeing.

Basic topics of a constellation

Set a boundary

I can still hear the pop today when Dr. Victor Chu crashed the baton to the floor during my first constellation. Demarcation - that word changed my life.

Setting boundaries, that was actually the solution. Within the constellation I was asked to ask my mother for what I needed and wanted from her. Nothing, nothing I want from her, I just want her to let me live my life in peace.

Setting boundaries, not only towards my mother: wherever difficulties arose in my life, I thought about where and in what way I could demarcate myself, and bit by bit my difficulties were solved.

Setting a boundary - forgiveness, how can this be reconciled?

For years, because of a misunderstanding of forgiveness, I gave my mother permission to "trample" in my life and destroy what I was building over and over again. Forgiveness for me mistakenly meant always reaching out to the other person for whatever they allowed themselves to do. Because of this false view of forgiveness, I was completely at my mother's mercy over and over again. It gave her the opportunity and the power to pass on her own hurts to me.

Setting boundaries as a solution in a constellation:

When there is an unresolved conflict situation within a family system, the pain, anger or longing passes on to the next generation. That which is experienced and does not find resolution in one's own life passes on to the next generation. A transference happens: The victim becomes the perpetrator and the pattern repeats itself.

With the, this transmission is stopped. The perpetrator is now thrown back on himself, he can no longer pass on his burden. With dissociation he is challenged to deal with his own pain, his own anger or his own longing. Delimitation stops what has been passed down for generations. With delimitation, God is given space to bring healing into the life of the father/mother or those who have taken over their role.

But the boundaries also have consequences for the participant of the process. Since he no longer has to deal with the mother or father all the time, he is now challenged to allow the pain, the anger, the longing within himself, to deal with it and to let God heal him. It is about getting in touch with one's own anger, one's own pain, one's own longing, giving them space. The next step, to round off the process, is about putting your emotions into words and expressing them to a counselor. Here, at this place, at the end of a long process, is where forgiveness belongs in order to experience deep inner healing. Only through the boundary deep inner healing is possible on both sides. Only from the distance, slowly and on a good foundation, is a new encounter possible and that takes time.

My own experience in this area:

It is not always easy to set boundaries for my mother. If I notice that she crosses a boundary I have set, I get out of the situation before it escalates like it used to. If conversations arise during a visit with her that I don't want, I get up and say goodbye! Over time, our interactions became different. For me, the situations improved and ultimately the interaction became better and more enriching for everyone in the family.

What does demarcation from the mother have to do with the question?

What we experience in our family of origin, we repeat again in our later relationships in the same way. If we have good and healthy experiences, we also live this out in our later relationships.

If a "trauma" is passed on within the family of origin, and such conflicts of origin are often "Traumas", we also live out these conflicts in all our relationships. Be it in our working life, in our circle of acquaintances and friends or among our siblings. We always choose people to experience exactly what we have already experienced within our family of origin. Family constellations show again and again that partnerships reflect what we experienced in childhood. We feel the same fate of the other and that is why we choose him as a partner. We feel understood in what is familiar to us in the other, in what seems to be secure.

Therefore, in all other relationships, boundaries is also required as a means of resolving the difficulties. Demarcation does not mean separation, be it from the partner, from the job, from friends or siblings. Demarcation means to create a clear distance and to make clear that things cannot continue in the way they were before. To stop what goes on from the other to me, to no longer be willing to be the scapegoat for others. Dissociation also means to get out of unhealthy relationships and to build new, good and sustainable relationships.

When one person leaves the system, the whole system changes. Through demarcation something comes into motion, the system begins to move again, to "set it right". The mobile, which is pulled by a thread, starts to move, wobbles and comes back into balance with all its components in a different position. It can never come to rest again in exactly the same physical position. Healing in this way is not time-limited or confined to one area, healing permeates the whole of the body," the whole web of the family system.

I believe that God wants healed and healthy family systems. HE does not only work on the surface, HE creates fundamental change. HE is first of all concerned about every single person, but in this context also about the whole family, the whole family system. This comes to me in the bible passage "Believe in Jesus Christ and you and your whole house (family) will be saved" (Acts 16:31). When healing happens in one person, God also has the chance to reach the hearts of the other family members.

God wants HIS healing to flow into families and I think family constellation is a good tool for that.

Proximity and Distance

Love your neighbor as yourself, and
you will do well.
(James 2:8)

We humans are designed for relationship. Relationship with our creator and relationship with our fellow humans. A healthy relationship needs a balance of closeness and distance.

Proximity:

We humans need closeness. It gives us safety, security and the possibility to let go. I am allowed to be myself, to be as I am. This in turn gives me security and trust, allows me to be open for myself and also for others. We humans need closeness to strengthen us for everyday life.

Too close:

However, too much closeness leads to dependence, it stifles and leads to the loss of one's own personality. No distance is possible. A sign of too much closeness is when nothing works without the other person, when the inability to do something alone becomes apparent. It is difficult to endure being alone, let alone to be aware of oneself.

Healthy Distance:

Just as we humans need closeness, we also need distance in order to be able to develop freely. At a distance, you can better understand things, gain an overview and also get a different perspective on things.

Too much distance:

Too much distance is expressed in the fact that there is no emotional exchange, no closeness. One does not talk about feelings, about what actually occupies me. The exchange takes place on the level of the mind, one exchanges about projects, but not about feelings. Too much distance leads to indifference, apathy, speechlessness and isolation.

Proximity and distance in family constellations:

Proximity and distance are a part of constellation work. They show the position of the individual family members and express how the family members relate to each other. Where is a boundary is needed so that healthy relationships can develop? Where are blockades that do not allow healthy closeness? What prevents individual family members from finding each other? Family constellations uncover an imbalance in these points and make it possible to find the individually appropriate position in the structure. It enables everyone to achieve a systemic as well as personal balance.

Shame

Healthy shame has a protective function. It protects the core of our being, the innermost part of our humanity. Shame can be well explained by the image of a house with a front garden and a protective fence:

The house is the core of our being, the inside of our being. The core of our being is that which makes up my personality. In Proverbs 4:23 this core is called the heart: "More than all else, guard your heart, for from it comes life.

Protected by the shame, the walls of the house, we have the possibility to unfold and live freely inside. We also have the possibility to look out through our window, to observe what is going on in the world and to let the sunshine in. In front of the house there is a garden, which protects us from the world outside through the fence, the pubic shell. Here, in my protected garden, I can plant flowers, develop my gifts and abilities. Now we have the opportunity to open the garden door and let other people into our garden. They are people we want to be close to, friends, acquaintances, sometimes even work colleagues. We even let very special people into our home, into the core of our being. Healthy relationships can be built when I manage to let only those people into my garden who are good for me and who help to develop my talents and abilities. And to put those who harm me back outside the door or even the garden gate. Here it is important to create distance again in time before they cause harm to you. This includes recognizing who is good for me and who is bad for me, and then disengaging and not staying in a negative relationship. This is the way to build healthy relationships. The walls of the house protect the core of my being. I myself may determine who I let into my garden and who I let into my house. Closeness and distance help me to do this. In the garden I cultivate my relationships, which are valuable and important to me. The shell of shame, the fence protects me and enables me to live healthy relationships.

Abuse

Abuse is like a combine that tears down the fence of my life and runs over the plants of the garden. Abuse can happen in many different ways:

Physical abuse:

This includes beatings, i.e. physical violence. The other, weaker one is physically inferior to me, at my mercy. Also screaming, shaking counts in this area!

Emotional abuse:

Emotional abuse takes place, for example, when I as an adult use the child for my needs. Children are not the pastors or substitute partners of their parents. There are things that belong in the adult realm, parents must not burden their children with everything that occupies them and thus overburden them. Adults need their own sharing partners! It is also important that children have the opportunity to develop freely, to make friends outside the family.

Sexual abuse:

Our sexuality is the most intimate part of our humanity. It must be protected in a special way. If sexual abuse occurs within one's own family system, the effects are particularly devastating. In my eyes, the current gender policy of already educating children in kindergartens is also a border crossing. To confront children in an early age with homosexuality, hanging up comic posters with sexual content everywhere, is a border crossing in the sexual area. Instead of protecting children, they are exposed to a sexualized atmosphere.

Spiritual abuse:

In churches and congregations spiritual abuse can be found again and again. When the guidelines and values of a spiritual leadership are in the center and not the personal relationship to Jesus, there is the danger of spiritual abuse. I once heard the statement, "Earrings or dancing are of the devil". It is not the things that are bad, it is in what way we use them that matters. Dancing is a very beautiful thing, I can enjoy it in a good way. Earrings, jewelry - God has put in us women the desire to be beautiful, we can use that. Television, mobile phones, PCs are an enrichment, as long as we use them responsibly.

Abuse, in any way, destroys the garden of our lives. Now that there is no fence, we regrettably experience people who are not good to us trampling in our garden. The shame that used to protect us becomes a wall because of this boundary violation. It is built around the core of our being to protect it. But since a wall is not permeable and does not have a door like the house, the person behind it is lonely and trapped.

Perpetrator (Täter) – Victim (Opfer)

In a healthy intimacy, two cores of being meet and form a unity. The exchange is voluntary.

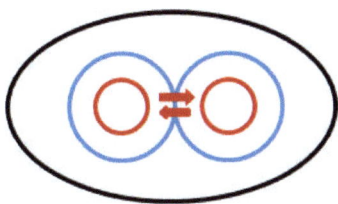

Abuse is an involuntary intimacy. The abuser enters into the core of the victim's being. The victim absorbs everything from the abuser and vice versa.

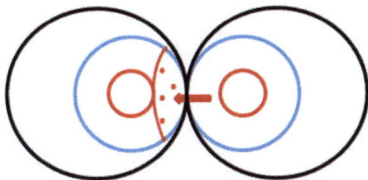

Every human being carries perpetrator parts like anger (Wut), power (Macht), satisfaction (Befriedigung) and hate (Hass) as well as victim parts like fear (Angst), fainting (Ohnmacht), pain (Schmerz) and love (Liebe). Everyone who acts powerfully, also carries a powerless person inside.

Opfer — Angst, Ohnmacht, Schmerz, Liebe | Wut, Macht, Befriedigung, Hass — Täter

When a boundary is crossed, the victim represses his victim parts and splits them off from his personality. In order to feel complete, he in turn looks for a victim and thus becomes a perpetrator. The victim in turn looks for the perpetrator's part in the other in order to also find his or her completeness. Victim and perpetrator really attract each other.

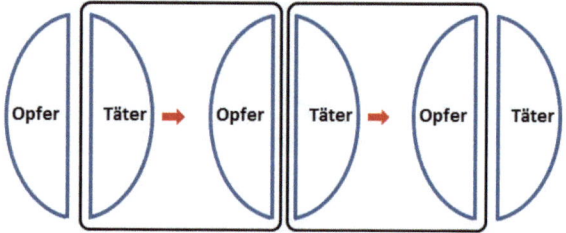

Resolution happens in two ways. One is to face one's own pain, to get in touch with one's own hurts and to face them.

Secondly, a demarcation is necessary. The demarcation from the perpetrator makes it possible for the victim to also demarcate himself from people who are not good for him. Through demarcation there is the possibility to let good and healthy relationships develop.

Violence

Violence has many faces. It is an act against the will of the other with the aim to hurt, humiliate or exclude. It does not happen by chance. Those who use violence do so intentionally, with the aim of achieving a specific goal. The perpetrators are those from whom the violence originates.

For the one who has to suffer violence, violence is always very painful, not only because it hurts physically, but also because it hurts the soul. The emotional pain can be greater and more far-reaching than the physical pain.

In groups, primarily in the workplace, in recreational groups, as well as in family dynamics, one can find a hierarchy of violence.

Hierarchy of violence

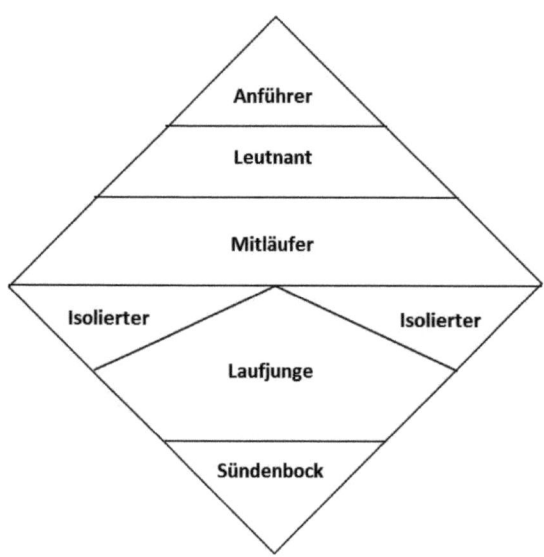

Leader (Anführer):

The perpetrator, everything starts from him. He is the mastermind, but his actions are hidden, not visible from the outside. He does not show himself, he lets others act for him.

Lieutenant (Leutnant):

He is close to the leader, but also close to the scapegoat. He carries out the orders of the leader. This can be done consciously or unconsciously. Consciously, when his Acting is clear, unconsciously, when he serves as a "plaything" of the leader, so that the "game", his cause, is implemented. In any case, he is a person who is close to the "Scapegoat" is positioned that is directly related to the scapegoat.

Followers (Mitläufer):

They keep the game going. The sense of belonging gives them power. Since they are not directly related to the scapegoat, they are also not up for grabs.

Runner boy (Laufjunge):

Has little status, is the go-to guy, executes things.

Isolated (Isolierter):

They have no idea of what's going on. They are not privy to what is going on.

The guilty one (Sündenbock):

The victim who is excluded, marginalized and blamed for everything.

You can find more on this topic in the book "Confrontational Pedagogy" by Jens Weidner.

Projection

"Projection is the 'throwing out' of one's own weaknesses and faults onto others. By blaming others, we cleanse ourselves of our own sins. To do this, we identify 'guilty' people from the crowd. Then we separate them from the rest of the crowd, isolate them and put them at the Pillory" (Victor Chu, Rebirth of a Family, p. 31).

We project our own weaknesses, which we do not want to acknowledge in ourselves, onto the other person. He is the bad one, the guilty one, who needs to be fought. When we do that, we do not need to deal with ourselves, with our own weaknesses and mistakes.

Marriage - the coming together of two systems

*Therefore a man leaves his father and mother and cleaves
to his wife, and they become one flesh
(Genesis 2:24)*

For a marriage relationship to succeed, there are three basics
needed: love, two systems coming together, and becoming
"one flesh."

Love:

Love can also be described as a relationship of the heart. I feel
drawn to the other, close and secure, connected. This is how
love can flow between the two lovers.

There are obstacles that prevent love from flowing between
two people. If I am still inwardly bound to a former partner, a
new relationship cannot succeed. That is why in family
constellations, former partners and former love relationships
are always constellated. Hidden things are "brought to light"
and clarified. Through this "understanding" the situation can
be dealt with in a completely new way.

Two systems coming together:

When two people find each other, two family systems
automatically meet. One is shaped by what one has
experienced within one's family and tries to live this also in
the new relationship. The "finding each other" of the two
systems means "hard work", but only in this way can a
relationship grow and become a sustainable relationship.

In family constellations we discover again and again that we are looking for exactly what we have already experienced in our family of origin, for example the theme of exclusion. If we find this theme on the maternal line, we can often recognize that the same theme also shows up on the paternal line. Children who grow up without a father look for partners who are familiar with this fatherlessness. It is also often the constellation of strong mothers and weak fathers that is repeated from generation to generation. The familiar attracts us. Things repeat themselves until they are resolved.

A Flesh Becoming:

"Becoming one flesh in the family system", that is the children. In each child we find a part of the father and a part of the mother. This part can neither be separated nor hidden. A child carries both father and mother within him. Events that both parents bring with them from their family systems unite in the child. For the child itself a new system emerges from these two systems of the parents.

Within the family constellation it is therefore a matter of directing the view to the two parental family systems and to track down and work on unresolved family conflicts there.

For children who have never known their father, something fundamental is missing. They do not feel "whole" and notice that something is missing. In the family constellations, this missing part can be brought together, the child can deal with the missing father and get in touch with his emotions towards him.

It can also be the other way round that the father, who has no contact with his children, clears things up in the constellation and clarifies them for himself. It often happens after constellations that new contacts develop, a new approach to each other becomes possible.

How a family constellation proceeds

Spiderweb

The easiest way to explain our family system is as a spider's web. Like a spider's web, the threads run from one generation to the next. If there is a knot within the spider's web, this defect has an effect on the other strands within the spider's web. It is similar with us in our family system. Events from the past have an effect on the present generation:

- War events: It was not talked about, repressed, but today's generation suffers from its effects.
- When siblings pass away, when a mother dies too soon, these are events that have an impact on the next generation.
- Family secrets, shame about something that happened within the family, can be such knots in a spider web.

The first Constellation usually doesn't reveal everything that's been going on in the family right away. You only get to see part of the truth. God knows how much we can handle, and he brings that out. Therefore, some things remain in the dark until the time is right.

For God there is no difference between present, past or future, HE is without time, HE is eternal. Therefore it is no problem for HIM to show and solve things from the past here and now.

How are knots untied?

-   Uncover, perceive and integrate into our lives. Knowing where my difficulties come from, recognizing and accepting the cause.
-   It is about clearing up things that have gone wrong. Burdens that I have taken over from my parents, I can give back to them.
-   Demarcation! Perpetrators and victims must experience a clear demarcation.
-   Victims need protection, support from another person and with Jesus accompanying .
-   Through appreciation: You are valuable and precious to me.

Practical implementation:

When I have complaints and go to the doctor, I first have to tell him what my problem is, what complaints I have. I have to describe to him exactly what is wrong. The more precisely I describe my complaint, the more specifically and concretely he can help me. This is also how it happens with the family constellation.

Then comes the anamnesis, the recording of the family history. As a constellation leader I create a genogram of the family, i.e. I write down the individual family trees of the family and the particularities within the individual generations.

Then the family is set up. The participant of the process chooses people in the room, representatives, who take on the role of the individual family members, and sets them up in the way they relate to each other. The individual persons sense the atmosphere in the family, together with them I try to feel my way to the entanglement.

Just as the doctor in an operation works his way bit by bit to the cancerous growth, so I too, as a constellation leader, work my way bit by bit until I come to the event that is causing difficulties. The wound is exposed. Once the surgical wound is exposed, the doctor decides how best to provide relief.

Question

The questioning, the formulation of the concern, is a central point of the family constellation.

Jesus didn't just heal, he approached the person and asked them, "What do you want me to do to you?" This is exactly the question the constellation leader asks the participant of the process.

The more precisely he answers the question, the more precisely he describes his concern, the more precisely he will get the answer by means of the family constellation.

Genogram

The family tree of the family is recorded in a genogram. What was the atmosphere like within the family, how did people treat each other? What was the profession of the parents and grandparents? What role did the mother, father, grandmother and grandfather play? Was the family affected by war or displacement? A farm or business can also be fundamental in a family constellation. Were there miscarriages, abortions or other deaths in the family?

The genogram gives insight into the family structures. During the constellation, the constellation facilitator can refer back to it again and again.

Family Motto

Every family has its own family motto, for example "Work, work, build a house". Work determines what happens in the family. It counts more than the individual family members.

Another family motto can be: "Boys are everything, girls count for nothing". This counted especially in earlier generations when it came to who would take over the farm or business. Even today, you can find this motto within a family system.

Taboo topics can be a family motto. In some families certain things are not talked about, be it money, sexuality or family secrets. Preconceived values are reflected in the family motto, for example "You are only worth something if you have studied" or "Women have nothing to say, the man decides".

The family motto determines the atmosphere, the interaction with each other, it determines the hierarchy and how the individual family members relate to each other.

Deputy

First the family of origin is set up, then the parents and siblings, then other important people who play a role in the life of the participant of the process.

The participant of the process chooses people who represent his family. He approaches people in the room and asks them, whether they would be willing to be a father, mother, sibling or himself. The selection of the substitutes happens intuitively. Often I hear the statement: I knew exactly that you would choose me as mother, father, brother or sister.

Unconsciously we choose the corresponding persons.

There have also been some studies done in relation to the substitutes in family constellations. The same constellation with different representatives in different rooms, none of them knowing anything about the other, always resulted in the same solution.

Knowing Field

How is it that surrogates sense the situation of the family? How is it that they know things that are only known within the family? How is it that they assume postures that the persons in question hold? How can it be that they pronounce words and phrases that the persons actually use? This can be very disconcerting.

Don't you know this as well? You come into a new group, a new environment and already you find yourself in a constellation which is very familiar to you. If we look more closely, we experience day by day how situations we know from our family of origin repeat themselves in our relationships, be it in our partnership, our circle of acquaintances, be it at work, even in our Christian environment. Entanglements that we know from our family of origin unfold anew, repeat themselves again and again, until we are ready to work on them, to dissolve them. And if we are not ready for it, we pass it on to the next generation unresolved.

What happens every day in secret is revealed in a family constellation. It is uncovered.

Primal Conflict - Place of Healing

The constellation work consists of working one's way from generation to generation up to the "original wound", to the "original wound".

"Primordial conflict". By this I mean the conflict which already goes back generations and which has been carried through all further generations. It is the trigger for many problems within the family. As a constellation facilitator, I see myself as a tool on the way there, as the "Helper" of God.

Having arrived at the "original conflict", I, as the constellation leader, point out the connection between the question and the "primal wound". By seeing the situation of that time, the participant of the process suddenly understands his whole life situation. It is like an "aha experience". He recognizes a connection between what was then and the present situation as well as his question. He gets in touch with the cause of his present problem. This has a very liberating effect.

Now it is time to come to terms with the situation at that time.

What was the person missing at that time? This can be the home, the missing father, the missing mother, the child who died much too early. What was missing at that time can be added within a family constellation.

Here, at the "primal wound", the place of healing, we are confronted with a wide variety of feelings. The released feelings need a resonance for healing:

- Lack of love needs closeness, a physical contact, a hugging.
- Fear needs protection, a foothold and security.
- Anger needs a space, the possibility to express itself. In a constellation it can therefore also be quite loud at times.
- Joy can be expressed within the constellation through laughter, rejoicing, hugging.
- Grief is the preliminary stage of letting go. Within a constellation I often experience how tears flow in a representative before he is ready to let go.
- Guilt must be recognized and repented of. If the guilty person (represented by his proxy) does not show remorse, he must first be confronted with his own history within his family of origin. If he experiences healing in his history, he comes into contact with his own guilt. This can all happen within a constellation.
- There is also room here for forgiveness and reparation.
- Shame needs protection, demarcation, distance and respect. This is especially true for assaults in the sexual sphere that occur within a Show lineup through "disgust."
- Pain needs comfort, relief, healing, attention and closeness.

The wounded person can be "re-fed", "refilled." God's healing is given space. HE can let HIS healing love flow into the family system. The family system is enabled to heal profoundly in a very short time by the addition of the missing aspect.

Symbols

In this phase of processing and healing I work a lot with symbols. It is a method from "Gestalt therapy". Symbols reinforce and clarify things. That is why I use them within my constellation work.

Ropes:

In order to illustrate pronounced exclusion, isolation, a rope can be placed around the person. This makes the situation even clearer and more obvious.

Stones:

Often, we carry burdens which do not belong to us. Burdens that we have taken on from our parents, grandparents or anyone else in our system. By returning a stone, we can symbolically return the burden that does not belong to us. Depending on the size of the burden, one chooses an appropriately sized stone. The receiver realizes, yes, the burden belongs to me, yes, it is not too heavy for me.

If the stone is not accepted, it requires a clarification within its own system. Only then is it possible to see one's own guilt and accept the stone.

Boundaries:

In encroaching situations, a boundary is needed. This clear separation can be represented by a stick or a rope. It serves to protect the victim from the perpetrator.

Ceiling:

The victim needs special protection, especially if he or she is exposed to a particularly difficult situation. A blanket can provide such protection.

Diamond:

It can clarify in partnership relationships, parent-child relationships: You are valuable, you are precious to me.

Jesus

Jesus is not a symbol, but when HE enters the constellation, the situation changes. Therefore, in particularly difficult situations, I take Jesus into the constellation as protection and strengthening.

Final image - Solution image

The processing of the original conflict already has an effect on the following generations within the family constellation. Piece by piece, as the constellation leader, I now move forward generation by generation until I reach the present situation. On the way back, symbolized by the return of the stones, burdens that have been passed on are returned. In the present situation I exchange the constellation leader with his representative. He is now in a completely new situation in which he has the opportunity to clarify things with his parents. Represented by "making himself small", he is transported back to his childhood and now has the opportunity to return the burden passed on to him to his parents or to tell his parents what he needs from them. In this final image, solution image, the necessary demarcation from father or mother is also very often shown.

The participant of the process takes this final image with him into his everyday life. His situation in connection with the "original conflict" makes him able to act in the present. Suddenly he can do things that were not possible before. He is challenged to have this final image present in his everyday life and to develop new strategies for action with its help.

A detailed description of the elements of family constellation mentioned here can be found in the book
"Rebirth of a Family" by Victor Chu.

My first family constellation as example

A father of orphans and an advocate of widows is
God in his holy habitation.
(Psalm 68:6)

My first constellation took place in a circle of friends. It was new territory for me, but it was this first constellation that laid the foundation for my concept of "Christian Family Constellation". With my friend Tatjana I had already exchanged quite a lot about family constellations, so that she agreed to a constellation.

When I asked, "What is your request? What do you want Jesus to heal in your life?", the answer came: "I cannot defend myself, I cannot say what I want. Others don't respect my boundaries. It is generally very difficult for me to show feelings". She gave examples from her life to illustrate her problems.

Based on her information, I created the genogram of her family. The family comes from Russia. Tatjana has a brother who is three years younger. Her father was a policeman by profession, her mother was an official in the youth welfare office and very dominant. Within Tatjana's family feelings were not talked about, it was not possible to say what one wanted or even to say "no". Similar things were mirrored in the generation before. Otherwise the genogram did not show any abnormalities for me.

I asked Tatjana to choose proxies for her father, mother, brother and herself. Tatjana approached individuals in the room and asked:

Do you want to be my father, do you want to be my mother, do you want to be my brother, do you want to be myself? Then she touched each person on the shoulder and led them to their place in the room. The people lined up represented the relational field of the family. It was noticeable that everyone was looking in one direction, that there was no relationship between the family members. Tatjana stood apart, separated from her family.

My task as a constellation facilitator is now to approach the individual persons and ask them how they are feeling, whether any bodily reactions are showing, such as coldness, warmth, heaviness or even the tendency to move to another place. I start with the father, then the mother, then the children by birth order. After describing their state of mind, I have the surrogates summarize the sensations in one word. The mother's representative showed clear reactions, so I knew that the constellation would continue in this direction. I again placed the mother opposite her mother, but they could hardly look at each other. When I now placed the grandmother again opposite her mother, the relationship seemed to be completely in order.

Now I turned to Tatjana and asked her if something special had happened in this generation of great-grandparents. Tatjana told me that her great-grandfather was taken away by the state and never returned. Her grandmother had a hard time dealing with the situation. So I took another stand- in, representing the great-grandfather, and placed him by his wife's side. There was an intimate relationship between the parents and the child.

This changed immediately when I asked the "state" to enter the scene. The great-grandmother reacted with despair when her husband was led away. Her gaze went only in the direction in which her husband had disappeared, she no longer paid any attention to her daughter. She lay huddled on the floor, shaking all over. I approached the child and asked what she needed. In its condition, however, it was not able to give an answer. I followed my impulse of "protection" and spread a blanket over him. The child pulled the blanket around him, but the trembling did not stop. What did the child need most at that moment? The father and mother who couldn't be there in reality. The father who was taken away by the state, the mother who could not be there for her child because of this fact.

In a constellation there is the possibility to change reality, to add what was not present in reality. So I put father and mother to their daughter with the words: "This is your daughter, look at her".

Immediately the child stopped shaking, lifted her eyes to her parents and shook off her blanket. Father and mother took their daughter in their arms and she began to "refuel" with her parents, to get what she had not received in her childhood.

This is the place of healing for me, the place where God's healing love can flow into the family system. It is a very moving moment when all of us in the room are allowed to feel God's presence and simply marvel. In a time lapse of a few minutes we are allowed to experience how a deep hurt is healed.

The injured person determines the length of the "refeeding", I allow them as much time as they need.

After the child was "full," she detached herself from her parents and turned to her own family. Now she herself was able to see her own daughter and give her love. However, this was not immediately possible as there was too much unresolved between them. Now this is where the stones came into play. The daughter (Tatyana's mother) chose a stone to give back to her mother. Since she received the burden from her mother as a child, she puts herself in the position of the child when returning the stone, i.e. she makes herself small in front of her mother. For the child, the stone is very heavy because for her the burden was also very heavy in reality. For the mother who receives the stone, the stone is not heavy, because the burden belongs to her, it is her burden that she had passed on to the daughter.

Now Tatjana's mother and Tatjana herself are facing each other. Here I exchange the deputy with Tatjana. Both cannot look at each other. Tatjana takes a step back to create a distance between herself and the mother, but this is not enough. I put a rope as a demarcation between the two. All tension falls away from Tatjana. Over the barrier she can look at her mother and meet her.

The solution picture of Tatjana's constellation is demarcation. Delimitation stops the burden that has been passed on for generations. Delimitation gives the mother the chance to deal with her own history instead of passing it on to Tatjana. For Tatjana, demarcation means that her own healing story is set in motion. Repressed things like anger, pain, powerlessness can come to light, healing can happen.

In a family constellation there are two places of healing: on the one hand the healing of the "original wound" and on the other hand the healing in the present situation.

At this point I would like to link the question with the solution picture. Tatyana's concern was, "I can't defend myself, I can't say what I want, others don't respect my boundaries. It is also very difficult for me to show feelings in general."

By seeing her great-grandmother's situation, Tatjana suddenly understood her whole life situation. She was able to make a connection between her question and the current situation. The grandmother was defenceless, she could not defend herself against the overpowering state. It was like an "aha" experience with a liberating effect.

Tatjana is now challenged to apply and implement this "end constellation" in everyday life, especially in difficult situations.

At the exchange meeting the following month, Tatyana testified that she can now do things that were not possible for her before.

Tatjana:

I have known Petra for a long time. She won my trust by openly telling me about her family situation, in which I found myself. She told me about her training in family constellations. I was intrigued and curious as to why Petra took so much time, expense and effort to pursue this education. Her narrative of ancestral experiences playing such a large role in her current life was too distant, too naïve, and too improbable for me. It seemed impossible to me.

When I received the offer from Petra to set up my own situation, I did it for her sake. I was skeptical, I hardly had time, but since Petra is important to me, I wanted to support her in her project. The evening began at 7:30 pm. Petra had already explained the family constellation in the round when I joined the group around 8.00 pm. Since Petra had already told me a lot about family constellations, it was okay for me to jump right in. It wasn't hard for me to be open, since I didn't know anyone else. I chose a topic that had been on my mind off and on for years. At some point I realized that I can't say "no" in many situations. It shamed me to tell someone my needs and wants. It was impossible for me to show my hurt feelings. When someone crossed my boundary, I was ashamed to show it to the other person. I allowed others to interfere in areas of my life that they had no business being involved in. I realized that my children were not capable of fighting back either. This was especially painful for me.

When Petra asked me to choose representatives for my family and to set them up in the room, I did this without taking the whole thing seriously. I was only affected when the representatives shared their feelings within the family. People who do not know me, my family, my country, my culture, showed our family situation in the depth. The core was hit, the true lack of relationship stood before my eyes, which triggered tears in me. I felt helpless before the unveiled truth that met me so suddenly and unexpectedly.

When the situation with my great-grandmother was presented, Petra linked the situation then with my situation today. It was impossible for my great-grandmother to defend herself, because the state was far too powerful, and she was also ashamed of her situation. Petra gave me a sentence to take with me, which has accompanied me ever since: "It was not possible for your grandmother to defend herself in her situation, but you, Tatjana, have the possibility, you just have to dare."

In the final picture, the demarcation from my mother showed to be very helpful. In the process, I became aware that I was also lacking demarcation in other areas of my life.

That is exactly what I have gained from this constellation. I can do things today that were not possible for me before. I have learned to get over myself and show my hurt feelings. I have learned to say what I want. I now recognize relationships that are not good for me and distance myself from them.

At the end of the evening it was clear to me that I would continue! The "unbelieving Thomas" became a "convinced and enthusiastic" one. Like Thomas, I have seen the reality that events from the past (ancestors) still show their effects today.

I have been with the annual group ever since and have experienced four constellations of my own so far. A lot has changed in my life since then. Things I didn't know how to change are changing on their own.

Conclusion:

God is a father to orphans and an advocate for widows. HE has seen the look on the great-grandmother's face when her husband was taken away, and the despair of the daughter. HE met these two in their need, filled their lack and gave healing.

Part II:

Topics of a constellation

*"How the diversity of people
so the diversity of issues."*

The apple of God's eye versus family structure

The Story of David in the Bible

Come on, anoint him,

for he is the one!

(1 Samuel 16:12)

David was the anointed of God, David was the apple of God's eye. His life was characterized by his relationship to God. God's anointing and blessing was on him. The blessing of God was on his life. God accompanied him and also brought him out of his depths again and again. He met him in his weaknesses and strengthened him again and again. But the more I looked into this David, I also discovered the chaos in his life, especially within his family structures. What shaped David, what role did he play in his family of origin, how did this shape him on his path in life and what influence did this have on his later relationships, on his wife and children?

As we can see from the anointing of David as king (1 Samuel 16:1- 13) he was the youngest of Jesse's sons. While Jesse looked with pride upon the elders, David did not count for much in the eyes of his father. When Samuel invited Jesse and his sons to the sacrificial meal (1 Sam. 16:5b), he brought only his seven oldest sons. David was ignored and forgotten at the invitation. He was in the field tending the sheep. One son after the other was presented to Samuel for anointing and again and again Samuel declared: God has not chosen this one. To the question of Samuel: Are these all thy sons? Isai, rather answers dismissively: The youngest is still missing. Look, he is tending the sheep.

David was not noticed by his father. Only when Samuel asked explicitly: Are these all your sons? Isai remembers that the youngest is missing and is tending the sheep.

Also in the story of David and Goliath from 1 Samuel 17 the status of David within his family of origin becomes clear. While the oldest three sons of Jesse are highlighted as they went to war, David is again associated with tending the sheep (1 Sam. 17, 12-15).

But even though David was not seen by his father, God saw him! He called him and anointed him king through Samuel. Even when he was denied the opportunity to go to war against the Philistines like his brothers, God gave David room to fight in HIS name and gain victory.

David was seen by God, perceived by Him and blessed. But not being seen by his father had an effect on David. He lacked the confirmation of his human father, the strengthening as a man.

God met David in his transgressions and hurts. We can follow the path as well as the depth of his healing in the psalms. They are again and again an expression of his healing and his encounter with God.

I know people with whom I can say the blessing of God is upon their lives, they are using their gifts and abilities for the kingdom of God and God blesses them. Looking closer, I discover a similar chaos in the relational structures as in David's life.

I think that there are two levels involved. I can, just like David, have a very personal relationship to Jesus, experience that HE blesses my life and uses me with my gifts. And yet, there can be very destructive structures in my life, which destroy what I have built up. It is the wounded family structures, which, if they are not dissolved and healed, break through again and again. Exactly on this second level, in our family structures and in our relationship structures, God wants to give healing. For HIM not only the vertical level, the relationship to HIM, is enough. He wants healing on the whole: On the vertical and the horizontal level; that is, both the relationship with HIM and the relationship with our environment, in which HE has placed us.

The role of the father

What I experience myself, I pass on. I can only be a good father if I was allowed to be a "son" myself. David was not perceived by his father. He therefore did not experience him as a father, which led to the fact that he could also not be a father and a role model for his sons. The destructive structures only became apparent in the next generation: Amon, David's firstborn, raped his sister Tamar, for which Absalom, his brother, killed him. Absalom did not respect his father, but competed with him. There was no trusting relationship between father and son, nor among the siblings. How much David respected his relationship with his son Absalom strained, the verse from 2 Samuel 15:30 showed, "Meanwhile David went up the Mount of Olives; and as he went up he wept, and he had covered his head, and he went barefoot."

The relationship with his father continued in the relationship with his own sons. The chaotic features of David's family system are also evident in the fact that the succession to the throne was not based on birth order, but rather Solomon was designated the next king based on a promise David made to

Bathsheba. Bathsheba was the strong one within the family, with David at her side who lacked male strength.

Children today have few male role models outside the family. In day care centers and elementary schools there are primarily only female employees. Many single mothers find themselves in a very difficult situation, as boys in particular need a father as a role model in order to find their way into the role of a man. But also girls need the confirmation of their womanhood by the father. If the father is not available, it is important for the mother to find a framework, such as scouts, rangers or similar, in which her sons have the opportunity to orient themselves to male leaders. The grandfather or uncle can also serve as a male role model and support the single mother. Family constellations offer a great opportunity to break through these one-sided patterns.

The missing masculine strength can be worked on within a constellation, a deficiency can be filled. In the processing of a "primal conflict" the missing masculine strength can flow again. A participant during my training once expressed it like this: What has happened changes, I feel my father at my back, he is behind me!

It is the same the other way round: Girls who grow up with a single father also need adult women as role models. Within a constellation there is the possibility to let the missing emotional love of the mother flow (again).

From partner to father

In a partnership, a man and a woman stand opposite each other. They are on the same level. However, this image changes with the birth of a child. From the opposite, the man now goes behind the woman. His task is now to protect and care for her. Very impressive for me is the image of the Holy Family: Mary, who holds the child Jesus in her arms, Joseph behind her, who spreads his mantle protectively over woman and child.

The man protects the woman, the woman protects the child!

Conclusion:

David, the anointed of the Lord, the apple of God's eye, bore deep wounds. He lacked the confirmation of his human father, the strengthening as a man. Also today   there are many sons and daughters who lack the confirmation of their father, who grow up fatherless. God sees them and wants to meet them in their "fatherlessness".

Take over the mother role

*Will a women give up the child at
her breast, will she be without pity
for the fruit of her body? Yes, these
may, but I will not let you go out of
my memory
(Isaiah 49:15)*

A wrong, not fitting role within the family system can cause confusion within the whole system. This is what Anna experienced within her family.

Anna:

I am the oldest of four siblings. Already at the age of seven I was responsible for my three younger brothers. Especially to my youngest brother I had a very close relationship, I was "mother substitute" for him and always dragged him around with me. It was my job to take care of my brothers when my mother was working. I had to help them with their homework and supervise them. My brothers were important to me, I would have done anything for them. I especially enjoyed the time when we had parties in our party room, which I hosted and organized.

My relationship with my youngest brother in particular changed when he got married. My eldest and my youngest brother literally split off from the family shortly afterwards, their wives began to fight and exclude me.

Looking more closely at the family system on my mother's side, I noticed that something was repeated in our family that was already to be found in the previous generation: the eldest daughter took responsibility for the family, the sons split off from the family, their wives fought my aunt. Again, there was a particularly close relationship between my aunt and her youngest brother.

At a festive event of our parish, a man approached me and introduced himself as my mother's cousin saying, "I belong to the split off part of the family."

That which showed up in my family of origin, my mother's family, already existed in the generation before. I used this insight for a family constellation, which led to the primordial conflict of our family.

At the time of the First World War, my great-grandmother experienced a great overload. Her husband at the front, she herself with six small children at home were struggling for daily survival. In the family constellation, my great-grandmother's representative used expressions and words that had marked my childhood in her insults to her children. The same wording, the same words. I knew from family history that when my great-grandfather returned home from the war, he was greeted with the message that his wife had died shortly before. My grandmother then took on the role of mother to her siblings when she was eleven.

Over the next few generations, this pattern repeated itself: my aunt took on the role of mother and I was the one who took on the role of mother to her brothers in our family.

This wrong role of the eldest daughter is the original conflict within our family system and the basis for many conflicts. The solution picture for me was the ranking in the sibling sequence.

About six months after this constellation, my mother

celebrated her 80th birthday. While I used to take the responsibility of organizing such a party on such occasions, this time I made no effort in that direction. At some point, my brother approached me and asked me if I would be at the party at all, to which I replied in the affirmative. Without me asking, he divided the four of us kids into shifts, all equally divided. I enjoyed sitting with the guests during my "off" times and celebrating with the guests and my mother. I took the opportunity of not being responsible for everything to take as many pictures as possible of the party and the visitors, which I had printed   that evening and gave to my mother the next day at our family party as a special gift.

This "taking responsibility" was also evident in other areas of my life, both at work and in leisure activities. Since I have stepped out of the "mother role" within the family constellation, it is possible for me without further ado, when offices and tasks are distributed, to step back once in a while and let others take the lead.

In January my uncle died, with whom we had hardly any contact. My cousin, unlike usual, called all the cousins personally and invited them to dinner after his father's funeral. At the meal, all the cousins then sat around a large table: a cheerful gathering despite the sad occasion, which only existed in this way from the past, namely before the break. Another cousins' meeting was planned. The knot is untied, the threads begin to tighten.

Conclusion:

Even if a mother forgets her child: God does not forget. He saw the need of the eldest daughters in Anna's family who were always challenged to take on the role of mother because the mothers did not fill it. HE gave healing and restored the order given by HIM.

Longing

And God said:
Let us make man in our image...
(Genesis 1:26)

We have a very creative God! When he created us humans, he put a piece of himself into each of us, combined with the longing to bring a piece of God's creativity into this world. We thus carry the longing within us to shape this earth, to make a contribution in this world.

This longing is dormant in each of us and expresses the diversity of God. If we follow this longing, if we give space to the creativity in us, if we live our dreams, this leads to a fulfilled life.

God created us as originals, but often we die as copies. What prevents us from living out the creativity God has put into us, what prevents us from bringing his diversity into this world?

In order to get on the track of this longing, I first have to ask myself who I am, what makes me, what is my longing, what is my dream. Or quite simply, what am I good at, what do I enjoy doing? It's not just the great things that count here, I don't need to reinvent the light bulb, but I can, if I like to bake, develop my creativity in it. Especially for teenagers it is important to try things and find their way in it. My daughter loves it, for example, at all sorts of parties and occasions to contribute a cake. Each time the cake gets bigger and more beautiful. She already has a whole photo gallery of her previous works.

Man was created to "create" something, that is, to pass on the creativity of God. It is not enough that we carry this longing within us. We are called to let it become reality in our life, to put it into practice, otherwise we are running after an illusion. This can also mean to swim against the current, to do things differently than it is usual.

As a child, we don't always manage to assert ourselves against our parents, we don't always have the opportunity to give space to our longing. However, we also run the risk of projecting onto our children what we have not been able to live out. They are supposed to live the life that we wanted so much for ourselves, and so the pattern continues, in that they are not allowed to live their lives either, but are supposed to live out our longings.

An unlived longing appears in many family constellations, especially if it has been passed on from one generation to the next. Her constellation showed me how much this is also the case in Monika's family. Her question was: Why can't I live what I carry inside me? The constellation led into her father's line.

Monika:

I had a pretty good relationship with my father. He was closer to me than my mother. I often think of the beautiful trips we used to do on Sundays in our family. A thermos was filled with vegetable soup, with which we strengthened ourselves on such excursions. I also love playing cards, probably because it reminds me of many Sunday afternoons with my father when we played "officers' skat" or some other card game. My father also loved to travel, one of my fondest memories was a trip to Rome together. How much these beautiful shared experiences have influenced me is shown by the fact that I also live out exactly these things with my daughter. We like to travel, do a lot of other things, and Sunday always includes a game together.

As could be seen in the family constellation, the whole family history revolved around our company. The weak men and the strong women who showed up in the constellation were always conspicuous. A conflict between my grandfather and his mother crystallized was the original conflict. He didn't care about the company. He carried a different longing in his heart, he had other plans and other abilities than those needed in the craft sector and he wanted to pursue these. My great-grandmother, on the other hand, did not agree. Her son had to continue the family business just like his father. My grandfather had no chance to assert himself against his mother. She forced him to take over the craft business, although he did not want to do so at all. Not only did my grandfather have to give up his longing, he also lost his strength as a man. Following his mother's example, he married a strong woman to whom he felt inferior as a man. This continued in the next generation, with my parents. In the constellation, a separation between my grandfather and his mother was the solution. Separated from his mother, he was able to rise up again as a man and also take on the role as a man within his family. The company was now no longer the center of the family, but the family itself. He was able to take on the role of father to his son, which had the effect of him being able to take on the role of man to his wife. This showed a new image of the family. The strengthened man who stands behind his wife and strengthens and supports her.

This Constellation had several impacts on Monika's life:

- Since that moment, she carries a whole new image in her heart regarding her father: a strong man who stands behind his wife and strengthens her.
- Monika has found herself in her grandfather's unquenched longing, which he could not live out,

and has taken it from him.

Through the "aha experience", through this "coming into contact with the primal wound", it is now possible for her to pursue her own longing and to put it into practice.

Conclusion:

God created Monika uniquely and put a piece of Himself into her. Monika carries her "uniqueness" connected with a deep longing within herself. She may now pursue this and discover God's plan for her life.

Farewell - Letting go

Remember not the past,
pay no attention to the former!
See, I am doing new things;
now it is starting. Will you not take
note of it?
(Isaiah 43:18 + 19)

A life of adventure, a life of blessings, a life for others, and yet the questioning of Egon's set-up involved a big why. Egon was an institution within an institution at his place of work. He helped many youth in difficult life situations and was like a father to them. After a difficult childhood as a "herd boy", his years in Africa, his education, his commitment to young people, he is now in his old age still very active, skiing, acting and can be seen at many a musical event.

His question for the family constellation was a big why: Why did my life turn out this way? Why did I relate to so many people, but not to my family of origin? Why didn't I take care of my sister, why didn't I take part in her illness and her early death?

The central point in Egon's constellation was his mother. She could not perceive her children because she herself was not perceived within her family. Only when she had clarified this within her family, when a demarcation was made between her and her brother, was she able to turn to her own family, her husband and her children. At this point the constellation changed. Egon was also able to perceive and meet his sister. At this point in the once in the constellation, I switched Egon's substitute so that he could meet his sister himself.

It was a profound and "healing" encounter. The sister had

tears in her eyes, tears of farewell before she too could detach herself from her brother and let go. After this encounter I brought the family together, who could now perceive and meet each other in a whole new way. It was a celebration of joy! What had not been possible in Egon's family before was now made up for. It was a mutual "refilling". In the end, the family had Egon's back, and he himself could look forward.

An important part of letting go is grief. It needs space and possibility, so that a real letting go can develop. What we mourn, we can also let go of. This is especially true for the death of a loved one.

"It's never too late to have a happy childhood," that phrase has stayed with me for a long time, and I can say, yes, it's true. When things are worked on within a constellation, I get to carry the final picture, the final image in my heart. Egon's lack was his family. He missed them, his relationship with them was filled with guilt. Now he may keep the new image in his heart. He himself is strengthened, with his family behind him. It is this image that counts and not the old and now past that he actually experienced.

I myself was plagued by feelings of guilt for years, as I had not always behaved correctly towards my daughter during a difficult time. I had cried out many times in my excessive demands. As I recently had a chat with her about the subject of "mothers" and asked her mischievously: "Well, and you, are you satisfied with your mum? After a moment's thought, she replied: "I've had a really great mum for the last few years, and I've forgotten all about what used to be!

I have forgotten what was before. Through a family constellation we have the possibility to exchange images in our heart and to carry the new, the healed image within us and to approach others in a different way.

Egon:

When I think back to my childhood and my mother, I was left with only two choices: Either to sacrifice myself completely for my mother or to completely detach myself from her to create my own life as I imagined it. Since I felt a huge urge for freedom inside me, I chose the second option.

After I finished my training as a typesetter at home, I left my hometown and moved to Stuttgart. My goal was always to emigrate, but my profession was not particularly suited to it. Africa had always fascinated me, all the stories of discovery, the great rivers, the untouched stretches of land. A colleague who worked as a typesetter in Namibia told me about the possibility of working there. After a successful application at a German printing company in Windhoek (Namibia) I could realize my dreams. I spent a good and interesting time in Namibia, but in the long run it was not possible for me to experience the local Apartheid politics with my life. The great longing for adventure and freedom led me to decide to cross Africa in a folding boat together with a friend. We put all our eggs in one basket with the possibility of not surviving the trip. It was a very formative time for me with many borderline experiences, in which I could experience the greatest possible independence and self-determination.

After this year-long journey, I was able to start a whole new chapter in my life.

Now I could tackle what I had always aspired to in my life professionally, the profession as a social worker. Looking back, I can say that things developed and came together during this time. Just as a mosaic forms a certain pattern, individual parts of my life came together to form an overall picture. People, especially youth, have always been close to my heart. The wilderness adventure developed into the human adventure.

Again and again I was confronted with the inner conflict that I had taken care of many people, but had neglected my family of origin. This had somehow remained alien to me. My work was a bit of a family substitute for me. Why did I have a relationship with so many people, but not with my family of origin?

With this question I went into the family constellation. The most central thing within the constellation for me was the encounter with my sister. In general I experienced a reconciliation with my family of origin, the feelings of guilt towards them dissolved through the family constellation on. An important chapter in my life could be closed, new energies were released.

Conclusion:

God has met Egon in his great "why" and has helped him to complete things in his life. Now Egon can say with a joyful heart, " I think no more of the old and pay no more attention to the former, for behold, the Lord will make new things, now they shall grow up."

Deaths within the family

Full of grief, she thought only of the death of her
husband and her father-in-law
and the loss of the ark of the
covenant.
(1 Samuel 4:21)

The death of a person can block our view of the living around us. We often experience this with dead siblings, especially those who are in close proximity in the sibling line. The loss of a child can cause the mother to lose sight of her other children.

Dead people must be mourned, dead people must be integrated into families so that "peace" can enter the family system.

I am not perceived

Gitte's concern was, "I'm the black sheep in the family, feel like I don't belong. What is the reason for that?"

Gitte's genogram revealed that both sides of her parents were refugees: her father from Croatia, her mother from Romania. Three of her grandmother's brothers were murdered in Romania during a Russian invasion. Gitte's constellation led immediately in that direction, too. Her great- grandmother was frozen in her grief over death of the three sons. The daughter's pain at the loss of the three brothers as well as herself was not seen. She stood apart, outside the family.

Here was the connection between the primal conflict and Gitte's position within her family. Gitte had taken on the burden of her grandmother, which she was also able to return to her grandmother in the course of the constellation.

A heavy fate that needed God's healing. I confronted the three murdered sons with their mother. The pain was great. I gave the mother and the sons space to meet and grieve. After confronting pain and grief, the mother was able to let go of her sons and let them go in peace. This opened her eyes to her daughter, who until then had stood apart, outside the family. Stones were exchanged, things were spoken out and cleared up. This had an impact on the present situation. Through the clarification of the former situation it was possible for Gitte to enter into her family. Here, too, many a stone was exchanged. The final picture was impressive. Gitte stood in the middle of her family, her parents behind her, her brothers and sisters at her side.

Gitte:

Through the local newspaper I heard about the open evening of the annual group "Christian Family Constellation". The Christian aspect appealed to me, since I also have a personal relationship with Jesus. After this open evening it was clear to me that I would also participate in these group evenings in the future.

At my workplace, in my circle of friends, I feel integrated and respected. This esteem, this respect I miss within my family, which is very painful for me.

When I saw the scene with my grandmother, who was also outside her family, I felt a great connection and sadness. I had taken my grandmother's grief for the loss of her brothers and carried it within me. It was a release for me to give her back the burden that did not belong to me. It was also very beautiful for me to witness my great-grandmother's healing regarding the death of her sons. My sadness disappeared and gave way to a deep joy.

The final picture was particularly impressive for me. Even today I carry this picture in me, my parents at my back, my siblings at my side. In everyday life, this image does not yet correspond to reality, but I can always recognize small signs that show me that our family system is in the process of changing.

Conclusion:

God met Gitte's great-grandmother in her deep grief for her three sons. She was allowed to experience that she is not alone in her grief and pain. He lifted her up again and made it possible for her to look at her daughter. By re- establishing a healthy family system even after decades, healing could flow into Gitte's family until today.

I have a good place

Deaths within the family was also Leo's theme. The death of his sister also had a great impact on his family.

Leo:

My sister died in infancy from a heart defect. She was not talked about within the family. In a previous constellation with Dr. Victor Chu she was the subject and resolution of the family constellation. In my current constellation within the year group she was again constellated. My sister's statement during the constellation showed me how much had changed in the meantime: I have a good place!

Miscarriage and abortion

For it is you who created my kidneys, who
wove me in my mother's womb.
(Psalm 139:14)

Miscarriages and abortion also play a role within the family constellation. They are children who were not born, but they are still part of our family system. They want to be seen and mourned and have a place within the family.

Miscarriage:

Losing a child, even if it is within the first months of pregnancy, is a loss and difficult for a mother. The body as well as the emotions have already adjusted to the pregnancy, are prepared for the child that is to come.

It is important to mourn this unborn creature and to give it space in the heart and in the family. Nowadays, special services are held for these non-viable children. In some cases there is even the possibility that parents may be present at the burial in special places in the cemetery. In a cemetery near us there is an empty cradle as a symbol for these children. Parents are given the space and opportunity to grieve today, which is very healing and good. The unborn children are integrated into the life of the families in this way.

Miscarriages used to be a taboo subject. People did not talk about it. So the parents, especially the mother, didn't have the space and opportunity to grieve for their child. There were all the other children to take care of. Or they were grieving so much that they were no longer aware of their other children.

In a family constellation these children are also placed. The reaction of the parents and siblings shows which important role they play within the family. In the constellation they have the opportunity to find a good place within the family system.

During my training, there was a constellation that included two miscarriages. One of them made the statement: "I wanted to live! When the participant of the process confronted her mother at home, she admitted that it was not a miscarriage, but an abortion. This allowed an open conversation to develop between mother and daughter.

Abortion:

There are often two possible reactions to an abortion: Either the mother is subsequently plagued by feelings of guilt, or what has happened is split off, often on the grounds that it was only a lump of cells. In this way, however, the mother deprives herself of any possibility of mourning. Often she hardens herself outwardly as a result of her split-off feelings towards her child.

The plantar wart

Hermann took the opportunity within the year group to put up his plantar wart. His question was: What does the plantar wart want to tell me that it is so attached to me and does not want to say goodbye? What does this thorn mean?

The constellation led into the maternal line: the thorny wart showed itself as an unborn child. Mother and unborn daughter embraced each other. The father, who was added, also rejoiced over the child. The mother felt an abysmal rage inside her at the death of her child. She rushed to the stones and took from them as much as she could carry. When she wanted to give them to the child's father, he reacted: "These stones do not belong to me.

From the genogram I gathered that Hermann's mother lived in the monastery for a short time and had to leave it. The reason for this is a secret within the family. When I, as the constellation leader, included the church in the constellation, it was immediately clear where the anger belonged. The mother gives her stones of anger to the church. That is where they belong. The family begins to regroup, the aborted child finds a place next to Hermann and his sister within the family system.

Not only the aborted daughter, but also Hermann has found his place within the family alongside his two sisters, with their father behind them, as a result of the uncovering of this family secret.

Hermann:

I have been suffering from a plantar wart for almost 40 years. Despite two surgical removals, it returned again. It has become a part of my life. Now I wanted to know who or what this plantar wart represents. I was deeply shocked when it showed up as my non-born sister.

I learned from my relatives that my mother had lived in a convent for some time and had to leave it. I can imagine that an unwanted pregnancy could be the reason for this. It was never discussed within the family.

My mother has always lived her own life. Her center was my half-brother Josef. With my father, who was much older, she had a marriage of convenience. My father was already 59 years old when I was born. When it came to her death, whether my mother would be buried in the same grave as my father was not coherent and fitting for me. This constellation confirmed for me that the decision was right.

Through the constellation I realized that the lost child and my half-brother Joseph occupied my mother's heart so much that there was no room left for my sister and me.

It felt good to find my place next to my two sisters, with my father at my back. My mother was distant from me, but I could let her be. Through the constellation I could now understand why she had distanced herself from us as a family. I found a bit of peace through this.

Conclusion:

Because the unborn child of Hermann's mother found a place in the family, Hermann was also able to find his place in the family and in life.
God is the one who created us, woven in the womb of the mother. He sees us and also the people who were not born, be it through a miscarriage or also through an abortion. They are part of the family system and want to find and take their place within the family.

Joseph and his brothers

But Israel loved Joseph more
than all his other sons.
(Genesis 37:3)

The story of Hermann reminds me of the story of Jacob and his sons. Jacob loved Joseph more than his brothers because Joseph came from Rachel, the woman he loved. Genesis 29:16 - 30:24 describes the story of Jacob serving Laban for seven years to receive as his reward Rachel. Laban, however, deceived him and gave him his older daughter Leah instead. Jacob worked for Laban for seven more years because he desperately wanted Rachel, whom he really loved.

The relationship between Jacob and Rachel was a relationship of the heart. Jacob loved Rachel more than Leah (Genesis 29:30) and this in spite of the fact that Leah gave him many sons, while Rachel remained childless. "But God remembered Rachel. God heard her and opened her womb. And she conceived and bore a son, and she named him Joseph." (Genesis 30:22-24)

The brothers hated Joseph (Genesis 37) because the father loved him more. The father only saw Joseph, who was of his beloved Rachel. He did not perceive his other sons. This caused hatred in them, so much so that they then finally sold Joseph as a slave to Egypt.

An earlier listing of Hermann revealed that his father's heart was also still attached to a previous love affair. His former wife died of tuberculosis during the war. His father's heart also remained occupied.

Both parents, Hermann's father and mother, were still tied to previous relationships and only got involved with the new partner on a mind level. This had an impact on their children. Since Hermann was not perceived by his mother in particular, he found it difficult to find a place in life. It is important for him to know: It was not because of him that his mother did not "see" him, it was because his mother was still preoccupied with her dead child.

Home

*Like a bird that wanders far from its nest, so is
a man who wanders far from his home.
(Proverbs 27:8)*

Germany is a country of migration! In 1945 it was the people from the East who came to us. They did not come voluntarily, they were "expelled" from their homeland. They had to leave all their belongings behind and start all over again in a strange place.

The ethnic German immigrants who have increasingly come to Germany since 1992 did so voluntarily, but they too suffer from homelessness: in Russia they were Germans, in Germany they are Russians. Their (grand) family structures and the close connection to each other give support, but also lead the members into certain dependencies.

At the moment it is the refugees who are streaming into Germany. They too have lost their homeland. They may be materially better off in Germany, but they have had to leave behind their culture and the family structures in their country.

The German welcoming culture touches me again and again. It amazes me how many people in Germany open their doors and houses to give the refugees at least in this way a piece of home and support.

For people who have lost their homes, this is a deep pain. This pain prevents them from living in the here and now to find and live a home. People who are affected by the loss of their homeland carry this unprocessed "homelessness" within them wherever they move. It also remains in the new place.

Through my constellation work I also become very sensitive to what people tell me. I recently had a very good conversation with my doctor in relation to the current refugee problem. In a side sentence she expressed her own life situation: "You know, my family has also experienced flight, we come from East Prussia. I keep moving around in my life and I just can't find a home." If this pain, this loss is not dealt with, that also means to meet the lost again, we pass the pain on to the next generation.

Emma was one of my friends who gave me the "Practice" of my constellation work made possible. Due to her move to Freiburg, she no longer participated in our annual group. Emma's constellation was about this theme of home. Her question was: Where does my "inner homelessness" come from? I have moved around a lot and don't belong anywhere. I wish I belonged just as I am, without achievement.

The Constellation led her back to her great-grandmother. In the great conflict, on the one hand, the loss of home became apparent: the family was very poor and moved from the Erzgebirge to Baden Württemberg due to economic constraints. Within the constellation, another aspect showed itself. The great-grandmother's heart was already occupied from a previous relationship, she was not able to give herself into the new partnership. The loss of home connected her with the loss of this former relationship. For she was thus not only the physical loss of the home, but also the emotional one. As an expression of this heavy loss and the desire to no longer want to live, the deputy lay stretched out on the floor.

Since family constellations are about adding things that do not exist, I first added the home, but realized that this was not enough. Only the former partner (who lay down next to the grandmother) in connection with the home (which stood protectively over both of them) led to the healing process and to the "refilling" of the great-grandmother. After some time the great-grandmother got up from the ground strengthened and was able to turn to her family.

In the further course of the constellation it became apparent that the grandmothers had a close relationship with their granddaughters, but the mothers did not have a close relationship with their daughters. They were virtually ignored in the relationship system. The mothers' anger about this was clearly felt within the constellation. At the point of returning the stone (Emma to her mother), the mother refused to accept the stone. Her impulse was to throw the stone at her daughter. After this statement, as the constellation leader, I asked Emma how she felt about her mother wanting to throw the stone at her. She expressed her fear of her mother and her hatred towards her. The mother's representative confirmed feelings of hatred and the urge to throw the stone at her daughter. A clear demarcation was urgently needed.

This issue raises another problem: The skipping of maternal love. If a mother is unable to develop love for her child, this maternal love skips a generation. The love that she had as Mother could not pass on to her child, she gives to her granddaughter, creating a rivalry between grandmother and mother.

During this constellation an additional problem came to light: If our heart is already occupied by a previous partnership, no heart relationship can develop in the new partnership. The marriage remains on the level of reason and is often characterized by coldness.

If a coldness between the parents is visible when recording the genogram, I therefore also ask about previous partnerships. In the constellation it is then important that this former partner is also constellated.

Emma:

The question of inner homelessness has been on my mind for a very long time. It seems that for me, "belonging" has always come at a high price, at the expense of my own aliveness. This made me cautious and suspicious in close relationships with other people.

In my family, I am a third generation single mother. My brother and I grew up mostly with my grandmother, just as my mother grew up with her grandmother. My daughter also has a close relationship with my mother.

In our family, moreover, there exists a precise idea of the social position of the family, many dreams of my childhood were warded off with the phrase: "It's nothing for people like us". A few years ago, when I confronted my mother with the fact that I'm a veterinarian and have a doctorate, something she can be proud of, she said, "Yeah, you, you've never been one of us."

I know from my mother's stories that as a child she suffered from her grandmother's harsh parenting methods and felt abandoned and unprotected by her own mother. I was touched to see that my great-grandmother's harshness was related to the loss of home and a heart connection. She was very lonely and with a lot of responsibility.

My great-grandparents came from the Erzgebirge to Göppingen as toy painters, where they found work and were able to earn a living. When they moved, they had three living children and there were at least three children who had died very young. My grandmother was born in the "new home" in 1912. From her stories I know that the customs from the

Erzgebirge always played a big role in the family. Still in my childhood there were wooden figures, smoking men and a doll's house from the Erzgebirge at Christmas. It touched me very much in the constellation to see that this loss of home has been preserved through generations right up to me.

My mother was born in 1938. She lived with a cousin in her grandmother's household. Their fathers were soldiers and their mothers, my grandmother and her sister, worked as maids. She told me that when she was a small child, she once went to her mother's house by train alone and wanted to stay there. A day later she was taken back to her grandmother's household, which was not a home for her. Even later, when her mother also lived there towards the end of the war, she felt abandoned by her. Throughout her life she remained bound to her mother in a mixture of ambivalent feelings. She was employed and left the upbringing of her children mostly to her mother. Even during my grandmother's dying process, she reacted with rejection and jealousy when affection became visible between my grandmother and me.

I always had the feeling that entanglements were passed on through the generations, a burden that passed from one generation to the next. Also thinking of my own daughter, I wanted to better understand all the connections and, if possible, solve them. That is why I decided to do a family constellation.

The degree of my mother's rejection towards me, which came to light during the constellation, shook me very much. When I returned the stone, I doubted whether I was allowed to give my mother such a stone at all, if it triggered such feelings in her. Wouldn't it be better if I carried this stone alone? The clear statement of the constellation leader that this stone represents the burden of my mother's life, which I as a child cannot carry at all, and the permission to separate myself, made me feel very relieved. It is still difficult for me to distance myself from my mother, but I am increasingly succeeding. I now no longer get caught in a hopeless web of guilt every time, as I used to. As time goes on, new opportunities emerge to hand over responsibility for her well- being or to let her do it herself. Allowing this to happen was not possible for me in the past.

In the meantime I have a trusting relationship with my daughter. I am grateful that we have managed to free ourselves from the web of entanglements within our family system and have learned to deal with each other in a good way.

Almost two years ago, I moved once again. Like any new beginning, the first time was very stressful, but the city where I now live feels like home in some moments. I feel comfortable in my new apartment. The climate at my new job is also warmer than it was at my previous job.

Conclusion:

By being able to recognize the cause of her homelessness, Emma no longer needs to wander around like a bird far from its nest. She is allowed to experience moments in which she feels "home" and is allowed to experience home.

Physical pain as an expression of the soul

When I kept my mouth shut,
my bones were wasted, because of
my crying all the day
(Psalm 32:3)

For people who have lost their home, this is a deep pain. This pain prevents them from finding and living home in the here and now. The pain about the loss of home can be so great that it expresses itself in a physical pain in the next generation. Physical pain often contains split-off parts, painful experiences that one cannot or does not want to face. The repressed seeks a way, it wants to come to light. Since there is no room for mourning what has been lost, for letting go of what has meant so much, no room for the emotional pain of loss, it shows itself as physical pain.

Heel spur

Gitte's constellation was about such a physical pain as an expression of a mental pain.

Gitte's concern was her heel spur with the additional question, "What is preventing me from moving forward, what is hurting me?"

In addition to her parents and siblings, Gitte also set up her heel spur. He took up a very large space and was at the center of the family during the constellation.

Everyone, every member of the family, was fixated on him. The heel spur itself felt drawn to the father. I asked him to stand behind the father, whereupon the father relaxed and felt strengthened in the back. I placed the two facing each other, where upon they fell into each other's arms. When I asked the heel spur who he was, he replied: home. With home on his hand, the father turned to his children and said, "Let me introduce you to my home." It was a very moving moment.

Connected to home and with his wife by his side, parental love could flow to the children. The final picture showed the children with the strength of the parents behind them.

Gitte:

For over a year I could hardly walk or stand. This did not go unnoticed by my year group. Petra made me the suggestion to look for the cause with a family constellation. My first reaction was: She is crazy, how can you constellate a physical illness. Nevertheless, I gave room to this thought and thought: "There is no harm in trying". The constellation led to the deepest problem on my father's side of the family, the loss of the homeland, and what this meant for my father.

During the constellation, I was amazed at how much space the heel spur took up within my family. Everyone was staring at it, it had meaning to every member of the family. When it became apparent that the heel spur was the lost "Home" represented, I could suddenly understand many connections of my family history.

My father used to tell us children a lot about Croatia. He came from Osjek, which is on the Drava, a river in Croatia. In the summer, we would bathe in the Drava, which often involved a mud fight among the children. A memory that was very precious to him was a day trip with his uncle on the Drava, from which they returned in the evening with a rich catch of fish. In winter the irons were taken out and strapped under the shoes to slide over the ice. There was always a great longing in his stories, even today.

This listing has created a great longing in me to visit my father's homeland with my children and grandchildren and to get to know the places that were so important to him.

Afterwards I took the opportunity to talk to my father about his homeland. He reacted with joy that I was interested in his homeland and started talking again.

The heel spur is disappearing. The more my father's home gains space, the more the pain recedes. The connection between the heel spur and the father's home can be felt physically.

Conclusion:

Gitte's bones no longer need to be "pine away". The cause of Gitte's pain was found. The body no longer needed to express the pain of the lost home. God has given healing in the depths.

Reaction to the constellation

This constellation caused a great consternation within our group, especially on Tatjana this constellation had a great effect.

Tatjana:

For some time I had been carrying a longing for Russia, but it seemed impossible to realize this. I was uncertain and doubtful, since my husband was also against it. When I heard the sentence in the constellation: "I want to introduce you to my homeland," I was struck by lightning. It became clear to me at that moment: it is vital that I fly to Russia and show my children my homeland. It was a confirmation from God for me. In Russia are my roots, my tradition and my culture. I confronted my husband, looked for a job to pay for the flight, and sorted out the day-to-day stuff. Then I flew to Russia with my children.

The absence of maternal love

He that believeth on me, as the scripture
sais, out of his body shall flow
the living water.
(John 7:38)

Be like an overflowing fountain, and
not like the bowl,
which always contains
the same amount of water.

In the first years of life, there is a close bond between mother and child. Mothers do everything for their children. Especially when the child is still small, the mother is required around the clock, even at night. It is maternal love that nourishes the child emotionally. Nowadays, men are stepping out of the traditional role model and are taking their role as father.

They increasingly establish a lively, emotional relationship with their children.

If the child is satiated by parental love, he or she will later be able to pass on the parental love received to his or her own children as a father or mother. Love can flow freely from one generation to the next.

A beautiful comparison for this flowing of love from one generation to the next is a "step well". If the top bowl is filled with water, the water can flow into the next bowl. If this is filled, the water again flows into the next bowl.

There are many causes that prevent the flow of parental love. Often it is unprocessed negative experiences from the past, from childhood, often even traumatic experiences that our families, parents or grandparents had to suffer through.

Franziska felt very touched by Gitte's installation. She missed this overflowing love from herself to her children.

The constellation of Franziska's family of origin showed that there was no contact between the family members. The constellation led to the father's family.

Also in this family there was no contact between the family members. The grandmother showed a terrible fear of her husband, the grandfather. She took refuge in the farthest corner of the room and cowered there on the floor. It was as if she was hiding behind a wall. She was only able to leave this hiding place again when I, as her guide, placed her parents at her side. They tried to calm her down and. However, she did not recognize her parents for a long time and could hardly believe that they were there for her. Looking at her parents was very difficult for her and very unfamiliar. For minutes, the only contact she had with her parents was to look at them. When asked if she would like her parents closer, a tentative "maybe" came, then she tried. Finally then all three of them took each other in their arms and slowly and barely noticeably some warmth and love began to flow. The grandmother was able, very slowly and in a way that was so unfamiliar to her, to refuel the parental love that she had been so deprived of. The refilling of parental love took a very long time. At first only a thin trickle made its way, but then it began to flow.

Having absorbed parental love, the grandmother turned to her family of three children. The grandfather, with his violent outbursts, was banished behind a thick demarcation line of ropes. So the three children could hug their mother closely and replenish the love they had been deprived of. A beautiful sight, full of healing.

Then Franziska's encounter with her father took place. At this point the substitute was exchanged and Franziska herself became part of the action. She embraced her father and enjoyed his fatherly love. Everything that was difficult between them was no longer important. She gave her father a gemstone and thanked him for all he had done for her and all he had given her for her life.

Franziska:

Feeling this unconditional, overflowing love as a representative in Gitte's constellation touched me very much. I also wish for this feeling of overflowing, unconditional love for my children in my life. Why is this not possible for me, what is standing in the way?

My grandmother was the youngest of four siblings. She was 12 years old when her mother died of cancer. Her father was unable to provide for his daughter, so after her mother's death she had to earn her bread in a strange family. She often told that she did not fare well there. Her father died a few years later in an accident on the farm. He had fallen from the hayloft. What was especially tragic, he was found by my grandmother.

It touched me very much that I even had to cry when I saw my grandmother cowering in the corner full of fear and loneliness. I myself had remembered my grandmother as a strong woman who had to stand with both feet in life. Now I experienced her in her weakness. Immediately I could see how the concept of strength in my life did not stem from any real strength, but was a compensation for a lack of love. My grandmother could not pass on love to her children because she had never received it herself. This is where I saw the connection to my initial question. I felt reassured and full of gratitude that my grandmother could make up for the missing parental love and pass it on to the next generation, including my father.

I was able to do. In the encounter with my father, I was also able to experience the love that had begun to flow through the healing of my grandmother's trauma.

My father and I met in a new way. I received a precious stone from him. His words were: I am proud of you. The gemstone and the words associated with it are with me to this day. I carried the gemstone with me day and night for four weeks.

Since then I have had several wonderful encounters with my real father. My children were also allowed to experience grandfatherly love anew. The relationship with my children has also changed since then. I am very happy every time when it is possible for me as a mother to live this overflowing, unconditional love that I have longed for so long in my *relationship with my children.*

Conclusion:

The cause of the drying up of maternal love within Francis' family was uncovered, and maternal love is now allowed to flow again. Angelica was able to experience that whoever believes in Jesus, streams of living water and living love will flow from his body.

Difficulties with children

That's why I'm going to keep doing right by you,
and also with the children of your children will I do right.
(Jeremiah 2:9)

If difficulties arise in the family with the children, it is worthwhile to look into the family history.

Leo's concern for his constellation was to set up the difficulties of his son Mark. It seemed as if Mark was being crushed by a weight. He found it difficult to lift his head and look people in the eye.

The constellation led in Leo's line to Mark's great-grandfather. He was generally sickly as a child and contracted tuberculosis in his teens. His parents, who were supportive, could not get rid of him - and release him into life - because of his illness. What was at first a support turned into a dependency relationship and the weakening of his personality. Bowed and looking to the ground, he stood between his parents, just like Mark. We had arrived at the primal conflict.

The weakening continued in the great-grandfather's own family. The children danced on his nose. Through a demarcation between the great-grandfather and his parents, a detachment could take place so that he could go out into life. Through the demarcation, a new power and strength developed in him, which he could now express to his children.

The deputy of Mark stood motionless and disinterested during the whole happening with arms folded. After the weakness in the family was broken, Markus suddenly showed interest in his grandfather. Are you cool! They walked towards each other and took each other in their arms. Markus was freed from a burden and suddenly became aware of his surroundings.

Leo:

I was always worried about Markus, because he seemed very depressed. I felt a burden that Markus carried with him and did not know how I could help my child. Within the constellation I felt that my grandfather's weakness runs like a line through our family system. Not only did I get an answer for my child, but I now understood the origin of the weakness of the men in our family.

I have experienced Markus as a completely different child since the constellation. When I watched him play soccer today, I was amazed at the freedom with which he moved.

Conclusion:

God turned the grandfather's weakness due to his illness into strength so that he could prevail over his children. Leo can experience that God is the one who works with him and his children, raises him up and strengthens him as a father.

Family Secrets

For there is nothing hid, that shall not be made manifest; neither is there anything secret, that shall not be made known and come to the day.
(Matthew 8:17)

Within the family constellations a very special phenomenon occurs from time to time: the "hysterical laughter". Yes, hysterical laughter, sometimes also contagious, is often a sign of exactly the opposite emotion: horror, speechlessness, helplessness, despair, hopelessness. Laughter is an involuntary attempt to discharge the pent-up energy. I take such laughter very seriously and prepare myself inwardly for an underlying tragedy.

I encountered such hysterical laughter in the constellation of Annabel. Her concern was: "I have a hard time taking care of myself, I have a hard time saying what I need, what I want and what I don't want. I attract everything like a magnet, when I say "no" I am haunted by a guilty conscience. Sometimes I feel like it's choking my throat. What's the reason for that?"

In "Primal Conflict," Annabel's grandfather stood in the room, grasping his throat and gasping for air, while his wife stood by with a "hysterical laugh."

<u>Annabel:</u>

Again and again I found that I was very bad at taking care of myself and my needs and standing up for them. When people around me asked me for something, I said "yes" - even if I would rather say "no". This was the case in all areas of life, in the family, among friends and acquaintances, in the club, at work. Sometimes I would think of words and arguments with which I would refuse a request. When I then faced the person in question, I could not bring myself to say the words, and yet I accepted. As a result, I found myself in an overload situation over and over again. Even though I knew and saw this, I couldn't change my behavior. Again and again I made things my own that were not really mine, that had nothing to do with me. I once said "no," I felt guilty. I could hardly demand something for myself that I needed or wished for.

The constellation leads into the maternal branch of the family. The key person turned out to be my grandfather, whom I never met myself, as he died five years before I was born.

My grandfather went into the First World War for two years when he was 16. According to what could be sensed in the constellation, he did this to show his family that he was strong, that he could do something. Maybe also to get out of the family whose expectations he couldn't meet. Later, he got married. The marriage produced a son before the start of World War 2 (1937). My grandfather fought six years in the 2nd World War and was afterwards still two years in Russian prisoner of war.

After his return home, a daughter was born. My grandfather's wife and the baby died in childbirth. My grandfather married again - this second marriage produced my mother. The marriage to his first wife was - at least from my grandfather's perspective - a love match. In the constellation, the first wife had a rather distant relationship with him, almost something contemptuous, as if she didn't quite take him seriously or respect him. She responded to my grandfather by laughing hysterically, looking at her son. The son's stand-in barely related to his father in the constellation and also clearly said, "That's not my father." My grandfather gasped, tried to say something, but the words stuck in his throat.

At this point I was able to make a connection between me and my grandfather. He was at a loss for words because he didn't want to lose his wife. He was unable to express himself for fear that she would turn away from him as soon as he mentioned things.

What touched me during the constellation was that my grandfather was the key figure. What became clear to me was that I had taken over from him the inability to stand up for myself and my needs and to take care of them. Within the constellation I had the possibility to give the burden I had taken over from my grandfather back to him.

In stories told by my grandmother and my mother, my grandfather was more of a negative person. He was probably a very unbalanced and above all irascible person who made family life very difficult. Although I did not know him during his lifetime, I always felt a connection to him during my childhood and youth. I was often drawn to his grave in the cemetery, where I talked to him.

My grandfather's story made me realize that if I want others to respect me, I must first accept myself. I do not gain the approval and attention of others by living to please everyone. When I make it clear that I am worth something to myself and I respect myself, I gain the respect of others. Now, when I am confronted with demands from others, I tend to take the time to listen within myself to see whether or not I really want to and can meet those demands. Sometimes I also try to connect inwardly with my grandfather. In the meantime, I sometimes manage to say "no" and stand up for my "no", although it is still difficult for me.

And I also manage, especially in family relationships, to address things that preoccupy me and that were always taboo before.

Family secrets:

Many families carry the burden of family secrets. There is a mention in an aside of an uncle who was a bit funny, an aunt who no one else knows about, but otherwise these topics are taboo. Precisely because they are not talked about, family secrets have a great underground effect on the family system. Not only do they take the direct route to the next generation, but they find their own paths in the family system. When such family secrets come to light, they lose their power and healing happens. I see family constellations as a God given tool to uncover family secrets, especially those that go back generations, so that deep healing can happen in family systems.

Conclusion:

God uncovered Annabel's family secret, for nothing is hidden from Him to be revealed. What Annabel's grandfather's first wife tried to keep secret was revealed. God not only reveals, HE also heals the wounds in secret and thereby allows healing to flow into Annabel's life.

The Wounds of the War

By his wounds we are made well
(Isaiah 53:5)

For people who, like us in Germany, have experienced two World Wars, many wounds have been inflicted within the family systems as a result of the traumas. Wounds that continue to bleed in secret. Wounds that are carried on from one generation to the next because the wounds were so deep that those affected could not talk about them. They buried the pain, the guilt, the shame inside. They buried and closed everything inside themselves so that no one and nothing could get at it. It is not for nothing that this generation is also called the "speechless generation". The children know that their fathers were once in the war, but what happened during that time is not and was not spoken about. Family secrets were created at a time when many people were burdened with guilt.

The saying: "Time heals all wounds", unfortunately does not apply in such cases. What is not uncovered, what does not come to the surface, cannot be healed. The unresolved conflicts that wars bring, that lead to guilt, shame, painful feelings, run rampant within families in secret and pass on to the next generation, often to the generation after that. They show up in relationship problems in later generations. This can be an inability to bond, depression and much more. Here family constellations can serve as a powerful instrument. Entanglements, especially from the war time, can come to light. Mourning can be given space, the dead can take their place within the family again, and a demarcation can be made from the perpetrators of this time.

War children:

War children are people who were born between 1935 and 1945, shortly before or during the war. They were still too small to be able to categorize and process the war and the associated destruction around them. So they have integrated this destruction unprocessed into their lives. It is not possible for them to name what they experienced, because they were too small at the time of the event. They have built walls around their hearts, their core of being, behind which they are difficult to reach. The chaos they experienced became a part of their lives, which they lived out as adults within their families. Dysfunctional relationship patterns are the result.

Many of these war children have already died, but the trauma they experienced in their childhood still exists within the family system. Their children in turn, the war grandchildren, lack any connection to the cause of what happened, because it was not talked about within the families. However, they suffer from the effects of the lack of relationship within their family of origin. Many find it difficult to find their place in life, as they lacked the basis of a trusting relationship within the family.

Further information on the subject of war children and war grandchildren can be found in the books and publications by Sabine Bode and Cornelia Kin.

Once the injuries caused by war traumas have been recognized and named through the constellation, they can be rearranged - the "knot in the spider's web" is loosened in the family system. We can and may experience: "through HIS wounds we have experienced healing".

Peace with the Father

May the Lord's approval be resting
on you and may HE give you peace
(Numbers 6:26)

Theresa's concern was to make peace with her father. Her question was: "Why did you drop me when I began to form my own opinion? I feel that if I speak my mind, I run the risk of not being loved anymore. I want my personality to be acknowledged."

Theresia's deployment led to the First World War. Theresia's father and mother clung to each other in mortal fear. They were trembling all over while the grandfather in military boots constantly circled them. He literally marched around the two. The footsteps boomed through the whole room. There was no stopping him, not even by placing several barriers around the two of them. Mother and son continued to tremble. As the leader, I tried to give them both protection with a blanket, which was equally unsuccessful. The boots became louder and more demanding. As if under duress, the grandfather's stand-in marched more and more vigorously. At this point, as a constellation leader, I placed Jesus in a constellation for the first time. The power collapsed instantly. The great-grandfather came to a halt. Mother and son stopped shaking and felt liberated. Suddenly there was peace in the room. All the participants in the constellation were affected.

My father was already 50, my mother 42, when my twin sister and I were born as latecomers. I experienced my father as hard and unfair, my mother as unpredictable. Until the age of 4, I was my father's favorite. I was a bright child. When I began to form my own opinion, he turned away from me and punished me with withdrawal of love.

A loving and close relationship had never developed again. He had no understanding for anything. If he didn't like something, he beat us up. Every time he spoke back, we got a beating. He used to say, "We got beat up, too, and it didn't hurt us."

I realized how far he was from me when we visited him in the hospital shortly before he died. He had told his bedmate about me as a little girl. He had obviously gotten stuck here and had not accompanied me in my growing up. I was now 18 years old when he died shortly after. At his death, in addition to grief, I also felt a great relief, because now I no longer had to be afraid.

This experience with my father meant that I never learned to speak my own mind without fear. The mechanism still works in me that I am afraid of being rejected if I express my own opinion. Through the constellation, the connections became clear to me, which helps me to pause and break through the pattern of the past.

When I saw my father in the constellation in his huge fear, all I felt was pity for him. He has passed on what he himself had experienced. He himself had grown up completely suppressed, an opinion of his own with such an overbearing father was unthinkable.

In that moment, I simply forgave him for what he did to me. Forgiveness was at the forefront of my mind. Now I could make peace with him. What a relief that was!

Conclusion:

Theresia had the opportunity to reconcile with her father. She could understand and empathize with why her father had behaved so harshly and unjustly towards her. Lord, you turned your face towards her and gave her a deep peace.

The horror of the war

He who does not let the guilt of the ancestors go
unpunished, but visits it on sons and grandsons,
until the third and fourth generation.
(Exodus 34:7)

Again and again I discover that the war experiences are not directly passed on to the next generation, but often skip a generation and show themselves in the difficulties of the grandchildren. I would like to illustrate this with a constellation during my training.

The participant of the process had a daughter who repeatedly had difficulties with other children. Although she was a bright and friendly child, she met with rejection from other children. The participant of the process presented these difficulties within a family constellation. It was immediately apparent that the difficulties came from the mother. Here again everything pointed to the girl's grandfather.

The grandfather's representative looked down at the floor, which in constellation work is an indication of a deceased person is. Another impulse was that this person was covered in blood. When a substitute for the deceased lay down in front of the grandfather, the latter rushed up to him, took him in his arms and sobbed: "I knew him, I knew him". The granddaughter's surrogate was then brought into the scene. She also rushed towards the dead man and gave free rein to her tears.

She had taken on her grandfather's pain and grief at the loss of someone close to him on the battlefield. The horror of war experienced by the grandfather was passed on to the granddaughter. The children saw the horror of war in the girl's eyes, which led to their difficulties.

As the participant of the process reported in later meetings, her daughter's difficulties dissipated after this constellation.

Conclusion:

Again and again it is shown that God does not leave the guilt of HIS people unpunished, but that the guilt of the ancestors afflicts them on sons and grandsons up to the third and fourth generation. But HE is a merciful and gracious God, longsuffering, and rich in mercy and faithfulness, keeping mercy unto the thousandth generation. He has turned the horror of war into mercy and given healing!

Traumatically induced Childlessness

***O LORD, what will thou give
me, that I should pass away
childless?
(Genesis 15:2)***

Traumatic experiences of war can reach into the physical realm, and Kathrin has many a story to tell about this.

Kathrin:

I had always dreamed of a large flock of children in our home, but it looks like that was not GOD's plan for us. Because of my years of due to the "continuous bleeding" that began six months after the birth of our first daughter, further children were out of the question. Rather, my life was marked by great worries about my health, even fears of death. All the doctors I consulted did not know what to do. All therapies brought only short-lived improvement. Only in myself was there something that wanted to know what it all meant. I still remember one evening before a hospital stay, when I was sure that I would now receive a fatal diagnosis, when I begged Jesus: "Please save my life and show me the way that leads me out of here.

Jesus has preserved my life and has taken me on a profound journey of salvation. In the meantime, my husband and I have been entrusted with four children who make life with us rich and colorful.

On the recommendation of my alternative practitioner, after six years of suffering, I registered for a weekend seminar on family constellations with Dr. Victor Chu. Beforehand, there were informative conversations with my mother, during which she told me a lot about my family history on my mother's and father's side.

In the seminar I explained my medical history, I mentioned the desire to have children only in a subordinate sentence, because it seemed too utopian to me in my situation.

We put my family of origin in constellation, that is, my parents, my younger sister and me. There was conspicuously no connection between the family members. It quickly became clear that the maternal family was to be worked on.

My grandfather was deployed in France during World War II. When he was transferred to the Eastern Front, there was a stopover where my grandparents could meet for a short time. My mother owes her life to this fortunate circumstance. My grandfather was killed in the war before my mother was born.

My grandmother, who lost her father in WW1, had to cope with the death of her three brothers and brother-in-law in addition to the death of her husband. Just a few weeks after her husband was notified of his death, my mother was born. The constellation revealed a complete emotional absence in my grandmother. The war trauma of my maternal family had passed on to me and expressed itself physically in the permanent bleeding.

The constellation revealed the intimate love between my grandmother and her fallen husband. They were able to meet again in their love within the constellation and express their mutual loss. As a pair of parents, they were able to give my mother all their parental love. My mother met her father for the first time and enjoyed being held by his strong paternal arms. The "refueling" in each generation lasted a very long time and was very intense and touching. After my mother was provided with strength and love through the generations, I was allowed to meet her. Here my substitute was exchanged and I became part of what was happening. I could hardly breathe with relief, great sighs escaped me with relief, as if an eternal longing was being satisfied, as if rocks were shattering. Streams of tears over the six World War I deaths in my maternal family alone broke. Tears that no one had ever cried before. The mourning process could begin and will eventually be completed. I spent what felt like hours refilling the maternal strength I had never experienced before. Still important was meeting my grandfather, whom I was not allowed to have in my life. Being held in his arms was such a wonderful experience. What was still decisive was the sentence to my ancestors: "I respect you in your destiny, but I leave it with you", which was visually clarified by a demarcation.

Finally, we put my parents, maternal grandparents, and maternal great-grandparents behind me. This resulted in a great strength in my back. The family was complete again. I can always recall this image and this life force to this day.

After the constellation, it gradually became clear to me that GOD had given me a new gift of life through the healing of these traumatic war fates in my family. It took another two years until the bleeding stopped completely and a completely normal, healthy cycle settled in. Then I got pregnant with twins. Isn't that a miracle?

I praise my GOD with all my heart, I will tell of all HIS wonders and sing HIS name.

Conclusion:

Kathrin was not only healed physically, but she was also given what she so desired, a large family. She did not need to continue "childless" after her first child, she was given three more children to fill her home with life!

Part III:

Further constellation forms

*"If you don't fight back,
you lose value!"*

Family of origin

Once the knots of the past have been untied on both sides, on the mother's and the father's side, it is a good time to deal directly with the family of origin. Through the trust that has developed in the meantime within the year group, it is possible to come into contact with the feelings and needs of childhood. Especially to express to the parents (substitutes) what I urgently needed and did not get. Clarifications between siblings or other close persons are also possible.

I recommend my participants to confront only one person from the family of origin. Confrontation with father or mother in particular often releases strong emotions. Further clarifications can take place at a later time.

Tatjana:

This constellation method was completely new to me. When I faced my parents, I was confronted with dealing with them and my feelings towards them. My mother had already been the subject in other constellations. In relation to my father, I always thought I had nothing to sort out, he was never there. But now I realized there was a huge amount we had to clear up. I told him that I didn't know him, simply because he wasn't there, and that I missed his fatherly love. He did live with us, but he was always on the road. Everything was more important to him than his family. I had the opportunity to tell my father what I needed and didn't get from him. I was able to work things out with him in that constellation, which was good for me.

Clarification Constellation

This constellation form is very suitable when the participant of the process has to clarify things with someone who is not open and not ready for a conversation. The participant of the process stands opposite the representative of the person with whom he has to clarify things. Where does the other person stand, what are his feelings? The constellation gives him the opportunity to confront the other person with his concerns without him being present in person.

Tanja:

I used this constellation form to clarify things with my former husband, which I could not address and clarify in personal contact. There are still too many emotions and unresolved things in the room.

When I confronted my ex-husband with my questions and feelings, the deputy reacted exactly as I am used to from his side. He does not take me seriously! Even a clear "no" he did not respect. Even a demarcation, symbolized by a rope, did not impress him. It took three ropes until the message finally reached him.

Through this constellation I realized that my ex-husband needs very clear messages. Since then I have been able to express myself clearly to him and to position myself.

Organizational Constellation

Today's working world is fast-moving. Employees who have often contributed to a company for years, who have built up a lot of things, become too expensive for the companies in their old age, and can no longer keep up with the "young" as well as the new technologies. With "measures" such as transfers to another region, with assignment "under-skilled and dull" work, through "Instrumentalization" of employees by superiors creates an environment that is not sustainable for some employees. I have been confronted with such fates several times in recent years, unfortunately also in the Christian sector.

Conflicts occur everywhere, whether in the world of work, in associations or in the private sphere. An organisational constellation is suitable for uncovering entanglements in difficult situations. It is about recognizing backgrounds, making connections visible, uncovering causes and also perceiving one's own parts. The aim of an organisational constellation is to recognize connections and to create the possibility to get out of certain structures and patterns.

While in conflict management only the present situation is constellated, an organisational constellation includes both a "present constellation" (present situation) and the constellation of the family of origin. A further level is added. With an organisational constellation one thus achieves a depth that is not possible with conflict management.

In the first part of the organizational constellation, the current situation is set up in a constellation. The participant of the process sets up the conflict situation in the room using a proxy. Each participant in the conflict then has the opportunity to share his or her view of the situation through the proxy. This helps the participant of the process to get a new perspective on the situation and to let the voices of the others have an effect on him.

The second part of the constellation is about: What is my part in the current situation? How is it possible that the other person could "dock" with me? Here I would like to refer again to the themes of "perpetrator - victim" and "victim - perpetrator", "Hierarchy of Violence". In this second part of the organizational constellation, the family of origin is set up. The solution picture of this constellation provides a concrete tool for further steps in the conflict situation.

Assaults in the field service

The following story happened to Stefanie. I was allowed to accompany her in it and am therefore close to the story. On the basis of her story I would like to explain the "organisational constellation". I would also like to include themes that I encountered in the process:

Stefanie:

For many years I worked for a public authority in the field service in the social welfare office/Hartz IV area. This gave me a lot of pleasure, because I have the gift to deal with people, to encourage them, but also to show them the limits. I enjoyed the freedom that this job brought with it.

I had the freedom to travel with a company car, to manage my own time and to meet a wide variety of people. I did not leave it at that, I didn't just identify "need", but also thought about how I could support people in their situation and how I could motivate recipients who were willing to work to use their skills. I developed projects to encourage the initiative of the recipients and to support them in doing things that were possible for them and to support them in doing things that did not seem possible for them. I organized removals, providing drivers and helpers "one-euro-jobs", thus enabling the aid recipients to make their own contribution. "My people" carried out apartment renovations for people who, due to their situation, especially their age, could no longer carry them out themselves. A particularly nice experience for me was when, during a home visit, I found an elderly woman in a completely sooty apartment. She had requested a new wood stove because the old stove was making her apartment more and more sooty. I pointed out to her that she was entitled to material for painting the flat, whereupon I got the answer: Good woman, what good are the materials if I have no one to paint my apartment? Two weeks later, this woman was living in a newly painted apartment. The renovation was done by "my troop". Another impressive situation was that a woman thanked me for her husband being able to work in my team, because through this work he would receive courage and appreciation for life again. As a result, he came out of his depression and no longer just sat at home and drank. I had a lot of freedom, which I used. I had a lot of joy in my work and has been welcomed by both the aid recipients, my "Work team", as well as appreciated by my supervisor.

The attitude towards my work changed abruptly due to a special home visit. An Arab family had requested a new mattress and I had to check whether there was actually a need for it. The man was home alone and led me into the bedroom. Already on the way there I felt uncomfortable. I turned back towards the exit door. He was faster and placed himself between the door and me, trying to kiss and touch me. I was frozen and in the first moment not able to move or resist at all, because I had not expected such a thing. The recipient of the help was so engrossed in his actions that I finally managed to free myself from my stupor, push him aside and open the door. Again he was quicker than I and again stood in my way as I tried to leave the house. Only with the help of a family from the second floor was it possible for me to leave the house.

I reported this incident to my supervisor and wanted to file charges through the employer. In a conversation between the aid recipient and my superior, he stated that he had sent his wife away (an appointment was made for the home visit) in order to "approach me sexually". Because of this statement combined with the vehemence with which the help recipient pursued his goal, I only now became aware of the danger I had actually been in. My supervisor told me this with a "hysterical laugh".

For a long time I misinterpreted my supervisor's hysterical laughter. I assumed he was making fun of the situation, but just the opposite was true. Through family constellations I have learned: a hysterical laugh that is not appropriate to the situation points to "tragic" situations. Hysterical laughter expresses helplessness in the situation.

My concern raised that charges be filed through the employer was not heard. The matter was swept under the carpet. I suppressed this incident as well as the experience that even as an official I have no protection in my job, as well as the experience that I have no backing from my supervisor. This triggered a work rage in me. I performed inhuman things until a total breakdown triggered by three further assaults!

During one of the assaults I got into a situation in which I assumed that I would not get out of the situation alive. I experienced a "fear of death" in real terms. I went through the same situation as with the Arab aid recipient, only I was aware *that there was no neighbor who could help me out of the situation, as the house where the home visit was carried out was very remote.*

From a subsequent stay at a health resort, I wrote a letter to my supervisor about the way in which the whole incidents had affected me. I informed him that I no longer wanted to work in the field in the future, but again I was not heard.

A new colleague was hired, but the field work for me continued. I kept an eye out for another position within the agency, but found that there were no equivalent positions in my pay grade.

I struggled through another two years, during which my body refused more and more and showed this through various blockages. At times I fought against a nasal cavity infection, which always erupted when I entered my workplace. After a stay at a health resort I suddenly could no longer walk, at that time I assumed that I had a pinched nerve. Other complaints arose, but I never connected them with the assaults. At the same time, there was increasing tension with my supervisor because of my many days of absence. Negative remarks on his part about me in the secretarial area led to a difficult working situation. A medical certificate confirmed that I could not reasonably be expected to continue working at this workplace for health reasons.

The certificate was ignored by my superior as well as by the personnel office. Attempts to apply for another job were blocked, as was additional training. During discussions about my future, I was repeatedly told that there was no other job for me than field service.

I looked for a job in the secretariat of a school within the authority on my own initiative. I enjoyed the work and also felt comfortable in the teaching team. During the time at the school, a new position was created within the authority.

I started a "security survey." Repressed things came to light, I got in touch with my traumatic experiences again. I submitted my experiences and began to work through what had happened. Three weeks later I was summoned to the personnel office. I was told that as of January of the following year I would be reassigned to the field service because there was a vacancy there.

I was only able to avert this with legal assistance. What I could not avert was the transfer back to my former area of work. I accepted the challenge, which for me practically meant facing my "trauma". I had a good companion who specialized in the area of "trauma" to guide me through this time. After I had found ground under my feet again, I took new courage and looked around for a job that suited me. However, I again had to make the experience that any effort on my part was blocked.

I also remained responsible for filing and data entry. I found this job very difficult as I am someone who likes to be in contact with people. Due to vested rights, my salary remained the same, which in turn caused tension in my work environment. My supervisor kept telling me that he wanted me gone. Applications for jobs that matched my personality, my skills and also my qualifications were not considered, indeed I was even told that I was not intended for such jobs.

Constellation of the situation

Stefanie took the opportunity for an organizational constellation with Dr. Victor Chu. She set up the situation of her workplace. Her question was:

"Why am I not being heard? Why am I not taken seriously in my situation? Why aren't they giving me a job on the inside? After all, there is actually a reason why I don't want to be and can't be in the field anymore!"

Conflict level

First, the situation was set up between the personnel office, the supervisor and Stefanie. Before long, the situation was in the room, which Stefanie knew very well. No one was interested in her concerns, the personnel office manager reacted annoyed. Stefanie was simply not heard.

Reprocessing with the perpetrators

The next step was a "clarification constellation". Perpetrator and victim stood opposite each other. For each individual assault, a representative met Stefanie. In this part of the constellation she came into contact again with her feelings from the incidents and thus had the opportunity to relive the individual situations and to express to the person what she felt in the situation, especially the feelings of powerlessness.

To the Arab aid recipient, she expressed how at his mercy she felt, how terrible his touch was, how rigid and powerless she was in the situation. She shared with him that this incident had made her lost her security as an official and since then she has been afraid that something similar could happen again.

She confronted the aid recipient, who lived far away, with her fear of death when he approached her after running around the room like a wild animal. She told him that she did not expect to survive this situation, also that the thought that she did not want her child to grow up without a mother gave her the strength to regain control of the situation. She confronted him with the fact that she was suffering from a massive physical limitation due to this borderline experience.

She expressed her helplessness in the situation to the psychopath, whose file was full of certificates about his condition, to whom she had been sent into the field without warning, when he blocked her way and insulted her in the worst way. She told him of the rigidity that has afflicted her ever since, the immobility that sometimes lasts for hours. She told him that at times she was still stuck in the situation and could not get out.

Facing the aid recipient, who chased her from the fourth floor to the entrance of the house, she expressed the fear he triggered in her, told him about her final breakdown, which followed. She told him about her everyday life, which she has hardly been able to cope with since then, about the impairments that what had happened still has on her and her daughter to this day.

The deputies of the aid recipients, in turn, had the opportunity to express what it meant for the respective meant that a public official was invading their privacy. In this part of the constellation work, Stefanie became more and more aware of the "encroachment" of her work activity. The "checking" of the cupboards, the "Checking" the hygiene items in the bathroom are boundary crossings. And these border crossings, which she herself had experienced in her life, she passed on in her field work. Her own transgressions were made clear to her. She imagined herself in the situation: A stranger comes into her home, looks in her closets and bathroom. It became clear to her at that moment that this activity would no longer be possible for her in the future, even after a good reappraisal.

This part of the constellation made a great contribution to her coming to terms with her situation. It was good for her, especially to face her feelings of powerlessness and fear at that time in this depth. In the meantime she has worked through a lot of this. However, she still suffers from the strong physical limitations today.

Family of origin - Own contribution

The third part of the organizational constellation was Stefanie's family of origin. She will never forget the final image in which her mother, in her own childhood, tried desperately to tell her parents about abusive assaults she had experienced as a child. They, however, simply looked the other way. Here was the parallel. The mother also tried to communicate, but they simply looked away, she was not heard.

With this final image in mind, it became clear to Stefanie: It's about being heard, being noticed in what happened and clearly state their concern about getting a suitable job.

A family constellation reveals things, brings hidden things to light. Now it is up to us to "implement" what has been uncovered. This can often be a very lengthy and painful process. For Stefanie it meant confronting the responsible people such as the personnel office, the head of the field service as well as the head of the authority with what had happened. Despite this, she continued to be reassigned to field work over and over again. No other activity was made possible for her. Only with support from outside, especially from the professional association, did her situation change. Today she has a job that suits her personality: she is part of a team and has contact with people. Above all, she enjoys her work and feels good!

Some time ago, she received a letter from the trade association with the sentence: "The incident is recognized as an occupational accident. Although the recognition does not include financial compensation, the letter was very important for her. It was as if a great tension was released in her body. What happened to her is acknowledged. What has happened is being seen. "I am being heard!"

Result:
- The responsibility for the field service lies solely with the responsible supervisor and not with Stefanie.
- Stefanie passed on the boundary crossings from her own life in her field work. Closets and bathroom are personal areas! From this constellation, she realized that she would no longer be doing this job.
- The central image of the constellation for her was the looking away of her mother's parents, which was reflected in the looking away of her supervisor. She no longer wanted to accept this looking away. It became important for her to name things and to confront the relevant people.

In an organizational constellation, the current situation is set up. The feelings as well as the points of view of the persons concerned are revealed. Often the hardening of a situation is also revealed.

This is also an opportunity for clarification. Not only Stefanie's own position is in view here, the counterpart (representative) has the opportunity to present his own point of view. This leads to mutual understanding and changing one's own perspective. Stefanie only became aware of her own transgression of boundaries as an official when the deputies of the help recipients told her what they felt during the home visits. Due to boundary transgressions that she herself experienced in her life, she was not clear, not aware of the boundary transgression within her job. After her reappraisal, a field service activity would have been possible again for her without further ado, but such a border-crossing activity as her former field service activity is no longer an option for Stefanie!

Her question was: Why am I not being heard? The answer for her was the final image of her mother kneeling on the floor begging her parents to listen to her, but her parents averted their eyes because they did not wanted to hear. Sexual assaults were a taboo subject at that time. That was not allowed to happen, so people looked the other way.

What is not resolved, what is not dealt with, what is not heard, passes on in the unconscious to the next generation and repeats itself again and again. The connection to the "primal conflict" was made. So Stefanie's aha moment was, "That's why I'm not being heard! That's why what I'm saying isn't getting through to the other person!" She found that this pattern showed up in other areas of her life as well. What she says doesn't get through to the other person or is simply passed over. She was fortunate to have a good lawyer guide her on her journey to be "heard," to support her in making sure that what was important to her got through to the other person.

Topics from Stefanie's
Organizational Constellation

Duty of care of the employer

The current refugee situation is a challenge for the whole of Germany. Authorities have to face these challenges in a special way. There are the unaccompanied minor refugees, there are the needs assessments from the Hartz IV sector, etc. Women, young, blond, often fresh out of university, expose themselves to a particular danger here. An open look, a friendly greeting can be misinterpreted by the refugees. If something happens, employers are particularly challenged. Are they really aware of their duty of care?

But the employer's duty of care is also required in other areas. Many employees are enthusiastic about their work and invest themselves wholeheartedly. But what about when they are caught up in burnout, illness or a change in leadership where the chemistry is not right? When all that matters on the employer's part is getting rid of the employee? Stefanie's situation made me sensitive in this area and I kept encountering people in such situations or people who let themselves be pushed out of the working world.

One side is that of the employer who does not fulfil his duty of care, on the other side the question arises why so many people defend themselves so little, which in turn is often connected to their family structure. As Stefanie's organizational constellation showed: on the one hand there is the side of the employer, on the other hand the unresolved "original conflict" in Stefanie's family. Because things in our lives have not been resolved, the other person can only "dock" and find a "landing place" in our lives.

An organizational constellation is a good instrument to illuminate and clarify things, on the other hand it also offers the possibility to investigate the reasons in one's own biography. What is the reason that these entanglements can develop in the first place? What is my part? The Organizational Constellation does not stop at the surface, it does not only try to clarify in the here and now, it also deals with the background, especially with how I can get out of the entanglements I am in.

Cultural Background

If we Germans were asked to draw a picture of our family, it would show a house with a garden, parents with one or two children, a dog or a cat, and so on. If you were to ask someone with an Arab background to draw a picture of their family, the nuclear family would be surrounded by many other family members. While in Germany there is a nuclear family, which mainly consists of father, mother and child, in the Arab culture grandpa, grandma, uncle, aunt, nephew, niece, cousin and cousin also belong to the family. That's why Arabic celebrations are much bigger than ours.

For us Germans, it is a sign of respect and friendliness to shake hands with the other person and look into the eyes of the other person. This is interpreted differently in the Arab world. There, people don't look each other in the eye, but at the ground, to express humility and respect.

The understanding of the role of women is also different. Especially for the "UMAS", unaccompanied minor foreigners, it is a challenge to find our women in the swimming pool in bikinis or otherwise in light summer dresses. They interpret the situation differently and classify the women differently.

With the different cultures it is like with different operating systems on the PC: they are not interchangeable. This is not seen by many refugee helpers. They assume themselves and their own culture when they meet the refugees.

This results in many misinterpretations and misunderstanding situations, which can possibly also cause damage.

The End of Stefanie's story

Stefanie's story still had a good ending concerning her employer. Shortly before her retirement, she confronted her employer again about the situation at that time. "There is still something to clarify before I leave". It came to an open and good conversation in which the superior boss apologized for what had happened. Some things cannot be changed, but they can be brought to a good end. As compensation, Stefanie received a paid leave of absence of 6 months.

Part IV:

Implementation
of the family constellation

*"It's not enough to know, you
have to apply it, it's not
enough to want, you have to
do it."*

Johann Wolfgang von Goethe

Recognize - integrate into life

Because I'm convinced
that the sufferings of the present time
mean nothing
compared to the glory that is
to be revealed in us.
(Romans 8:18)

In the family constellation, what was missing, what triggered the pain, the anger or the fear, is brought back. A reconciliation, a reconciliation with the situation at that time is given space. Things that could not be worked through in the situation at the time are given space during the constellation.

With this, one also comes into contact with the feelings of other generations. Repressed feelings come to light, I feel this anger, this pain, this fear that has been suppressed for generations, I come into contact with the cause. Now it is necessary to give these feelings space, they are allowed to be. This can be very intense and painful. Here I need people, friends, pastors, therapists, who accompany me.

The family constellation process is of no use if I do not integrate what I have recognized into everyday life. Stefanie was challenged to do things in order to be "heard", Leo is challenged to transform his previous weakness into strength and to assert himself in relation to his children. With Theresia it is about having the courage to bring in one's own opinion, whereby the other person is also allowed to have his opinion, without Theresia is thereby attacked in her personality. This brings movement into the system and movement into the environment.

When one person leaves the system, the whole system

changes. Something starts to move, the system starts to "straighten itself out". At this point I would like to return to the story of the Titanic at the beginning of the book. Breaking free of family entanglements is like Rose's sinking of the Titanic. A huge ship had to go down, many people had to die, in order for Rose to have the opportunity to break free from her family entanglements. Titanic was just a movie, but it showed very well how massive family structures can be. We don't need such a huge ship to go down, we don't need other people to lose their lives, but "getting out" of what has gone before brings a lot of movement and, first of all, a huge mess. It is an enormous process which is set in motion.

The fact that the journey is worthwhile is shown by the statement of a participant in our annual group: "Once I have entered the path of healing, there is no turning back. The uncovering may be painful, but it is also very liberating!"

"Ye shall know the truth, and the truth shall make you free" (John 8:32).

Implementation of setting a boundary

If I said something wrong, prove it to me!
But if I am right, why do you strike me?
(John 18:23)

Jesus could distinguish himself, even in the difficult situation of his imprisonment. He could name things, clearly stated what is his part (death for our sins) and what is the part of those who condemned him.

Setting a boundary therefore also means clearly calling things by their name. Things must no longer be swept under the carpet. Take a stand! What is my part and what is the part of the other? We can leave the other person's share up to him. It is his problem, I am not responsible for it.

If the other person refuses to accept my boundaries, I need support from outside, possibly through a good lawyer, who helps me to enforce this boundary. Especially towards my house administration such help from outside was necessary, and lo and behold, it worked. What is not possible for me alone, I can implement with outside help.

No longer allow boundaries to be crossed! Clearly state the boundary and if the other person does not accept them, get support from outside!

I'm not being heard

If people don't take you in and
don't want to hear your words,
depart from that house or city,
and shake off the dust from your feet.
(Matthew 10:14)

Not being heard was Stefanie's life theme. It is very closely connected with the theme of demarcation. Again and again she experienced that even good thoughts and ideas simply did not get through. That hurt. In her job, she was dependent on the income and the activity. Stefanie could not simply say: I'll shake the dust off my feet and look for something else. For that, she had the responsibility of a child and also earned quite well. In addition, she suffered from severe physical impairments since her breakdown. The incidents at her workplace were the reason for her physical limitations, so she didn't want to be pushed out. That is why it was so important for her to stay at this job and to fight for it. Today she is proud that she has managed to stand up for herself and her rights and to have a job again that she enjoys.

In her life's journey, she has learned to deal with this issue in two ways. Either to fight when the situation demands it, or to take Jesus' word literally, "shake the dust off your feet" and look for another opportunity. If she finds that what she has to contribute is not being received, then she may know there are other places with open doors.

It was not easy to let go, but I myself made the experience, if I do not find openness for my gifts and abilities, there are also other places where I can contribute. God is not limited, in HIM new ways open up again and again, if we go forward with HIM.

Conclusion:

There are areas in our lives where we need support to make ourselves heard. In other areas it means to look for new ways and new possibilities; often these turn out to be better and more suitable in retrospect.

Conclusion:

It's good to have courage!

*"And if we
are freed from our own fear,
our presence automatically liberates others".*

Nelson Mandela

Family constellations at a forge

Because you are dear in my eyes, respected, and
because I love you.
(Isaiah 43:4)

My friend Petra runs an organic farm with a forge together with her husband. At a women's evening, a joint "candel-light-dinner in the forge", a new project was born: family constellations in a special ambience, the forge. Six times a year half-day seminars take place here. In the meantime, a partially permanent group has also formed in this setting.

Petra:

One of my prayer requests has long been that GOD can use us and our farm to bring healing to our world. By converting to organic farming, we took the first steps in this direction. In the summer of 2015 we were able to renovate the old blacksmith's shop on the farm, which had been u n u s e d f o r years as a junk room. It quickly became clear that this was no ordinary space, this was a sacred place. In the meantime, many wonderful things have been allowed to take place in the forge, carried by GOD'S HOLY SPIRIT. The highlight is of course the family constellation. GOD uses the forge with its charisma to give us a trusting, protective framework so that the seminars can take place in a beneficial atmosphere. The culinary pampering program rounds off the seminar and compensates us for the often hard work in family constellations. See and taste how friendly the Lord is - that is good for everyone. The fellowship and the physical enjoyment help the participants to get back to everyday life and to continue the path they have started on in a strengthened way.

Together with Petra I started the "Christian Family Constellation". The time together as well as the seminars in the forge were a very valuable time. Unfortunately, Petra had to give up her cooperation as well as the day seminars in the Schmiede at the end of 2018 due to health problems. These seminars will now take place in Lahr since 2019

Our deepest fear

"Our most profound fear, is not that we are insufficient. Our most profound fear is being powerful beyond what can be measured.
It is our light, not our darkness, that scares us the most.
We ask ourselves, who am I to call myself brilliant, great, talented, fantastic? But who are you not to call yourself that?
You are a child of God. Keeping yourself small does not serve the world. There is nothing enlightened about making yourself so small so that others around you don't feel insecure.
We are all meant to shine as children do. We were born to manifest the radiance of God that is within us. He is not just in a few of us. He is in each and every one of us.
And when we let our light appear, we unconsciously give other people permission to do the same.
When we are liberated from our own fear, our presence automatically liberates others."

(Nelson Mandela)

I know this "deepest fear" from my life as well. I think we all struggle with it. Who am I that God can really use me? The image I was given by my mother did not match what God put in my heart. Time and again, when I thought I had found my place in life, a place where I could and wanted to contribute with my gifts and abilities, then "profound fear" and destroyed my life's dreams.

It is through family constellations that I have experienced a great deal of healing in my life over the last few years. I feel that I am in the process of overcoming my "deep fear", realizing and understanding that I am brilliant, great, talented and fantastic. That God has a plan for me and for my life and that I get to make a contribution in this world as a result. In good times we thrive, in hard times we grow. Just what has been hard for me in my life, has made me grow and mature, has prepared me for my task, which is now in front of me.

Family constellation is a tool, an instrument, but I feel that God wants to use me with this "tool" to bring some healing and HIS love into this world. Yes, I believe that HE wants to use me and can use me in a greater way than I imagine.

With HIS love I have my "deepest fear" overcome, I know I don't need to make myself small anymore, I get to be who I am and serve God with my gifts and abilities.

Courage is good for!

"And when we are liberated from our own fear, our presence automatically liberates others".

Dear Reader,

I have tried to introduce you to family constellations and have shared with you the experiences of our year group. I believe that family constellation is a method to easily get in touch with your own basic hurts and therefore those within the family system. I believe that God wants to use this method to bring healing into our families.

I want to encourage you with this book: Face your past and experience healing, and discover God's plan for your life. Find your place in this world and bring your light into it.

Sometimes you have to dare things to experience God's blessings in your life. God sees the needs of our time and I believe family constellation is HIS answer to that - our chance. I want to encourage you to try it.

My thanks to:

Victor Chu, with whom I was allowed to get to know this special kind of family constellation. I was able to experience him as a mindful and respectful person and learned a lot from him, far beyond family constellations.

Klaus Hettmer, who, like me, walks the path with Jesus, with whom I was able to exchange ideas again and again, especially during my training, and who awakened the thought of writing this book in me.

Petra Kehrer-Lutz for her friendship, her open ear, the exchange and the encouragement I always get from her. It is nice to build up this constellation work together with her and to go forward on this path together with her.

The year group as well as my two friends Egon and Elke, who accompanied me in writing the book and made their family constellations available. I am grateful for the beautiful and deep encounters during this time. Thank you for your openness and willingness to open up a piece of your life path for others.

Salome, my daughter, who read my first draft and gave me lots of good advice as a result, for her interest in my book, as well as her support - just for being there!

Sabine Anderheiden, Petra Kehrer-Lutz, Clemens Bühler, Friederike Hammig, Angelika Soth and Eva Bayer-Lay for proofreading the book.

Eddy Hangs for the graphics, Eva Bayer-Lay for the formatting.

Attorney Wolfgang Reichert, for his faithful guidance in so many areas of my life, for helping me realize my concerns, and for the legal advice for this book. Thank you for the many good conversations that have always taken place.

But most of all I want to thank JESUS, who accompanied me and gave me many thoughts for this book!

Appendix

Offers of the
"Christian Family Constellations"

Things developed over the years. Due to two broadcasts on Radio Horeb, I received many inquiries regarding "Christian Family Constellations". Groups were formed in the Würzburg and Munich area, which meet four times a year. The offered weekends can be taken individually or as a continuous group (process group). Day and weekend seminars also take place in the Frankfurt area and in Lahr.

Again and again I am asked about a training in "Christian Family Constellations". Since autumn 2023, I have been offering healing seminars in conjunction with family constellations. Within this seminars, suitable participants can be trained in family constellations.

For years I have been carrying the desire in my heart to translate my book into English. Again and again I looked for possibilities, but it could not be realized. With the help of the translation program "Deeple" I have dared to do it in January 2023. Thanks To Diana Mascarenas who corrected the translation in May 2025.

Further dates and information at:
www.christliches-familienstellen.eu
Video: Youtube Petra Bouren

Literature reference:

- Chu, Victor, Rebirth of a Family, Peter Hammer Verlag, Wuppertal 2008, ISBN 978-3-7795-.0204-3
- Bode Sabine, Kriegskinder und Kriegsenkel, Klett-Cotta Verlag, Stuttgart 2009
- Cornelia Kin und Angelika Henke, Kriegsenkel, Trauma erkennen, verstehen und heilen, BoD 2022
- Definition of violence: Wikipedia
- „Deeple" for the translation into English

Photo credits:

- "Cover" template Salome Bouren, painted by Petra Bouren
- "On the road together" Shutterstock.com.
- "The Wall" template Karin Swientek, painted by Petra Bouren
- "Holy Family" photograph of a South Tyrolean woodcarving by Petra Bouren.
- Three-shelled fountain in Maulbronn Monastery (14th century).
  Source: Nemracc / wikimedia
- The sketches "Perpetrator and Victim" are thought by Dr. Victor Chu
- Diagram "Hierarchy of violence": Weidner, Jens, Konfrontative Pädagogik, Forum Verlag Godesverlag GmbH, Mönchengladbach 2008, ISBN 978-3-930982-71-4